Romney vs. Perry On The Issues

**Jesse Gordon,
OnTheIssues.org**

Contents

Romney vs. Perry on International Issues 103

Book reviews 132

Romney vs. Perry on VoteMatch 140

Afterword 142

Introduction

Governor Mitt Romney of Massachusetts and Governor Rick Perry of Texas currently stand as two of the top-tier frontrunners for the 2012 Republican presidential nomination. This book outlines their stances on the issues, in a side-by-side manner for each issue, on many of controversial topics that they will face as President.

We gather the two governors' issue stances from their political autobiographies; from debates in both the 2011 election season and past elections; from public speeches; from campaign websites; and from political analysis websites. All of the excerpts appear, with many additional issue stances, on our website, www.OnTheIssues.org.

The purpose of this book, and the mission of our website, is to inform voters about candidates' issue stances—what they believe about the issues, and what they have done to implement those beliefs. The mainstream media report on candidates' politics: who's ahead this week; who "won" the last debate; who has endorsed whom. We reject the "horse race politics" that dominates the mainstream media, and instead focus on what matters: Romney on the issues versus Perry on the issues.

—Jesse Gordon, editor-in-chief, jesse@OnTheIssues.org

Dedication

To Julien

Acknowledgments

This book would not have been possible without the tireless efforts of the entire OnTheIssues team: Derek Camara, Janice Gordon, Michele Gordon, Peter Hoerr, Ram Lau, Jamie Leighton, Adam Leighton, Naomi Lichtenberg, Ogden Porter, Will Rico, Dan Teittinen, Irma Teittinen, and especially Kathleen Camara.

Romney vs. Perry on Domestic Issues

Domestic issues focus on joint state-federal jurisdiction or enforcement, including the following topics:

- *Crime:* including mandatory sentencing and the death penalty. During Perry's governorship, Texas executed more death-row inmates than any other state. Massachusetts has no death penalty, so Romney focuses on the federal death penalty.

- *Gun Control:* Texas has considerably less restrictive gun regulations than Massachusetts. Perry focuses on Second Amendment rights while Romney focuses on specifics of gun restrictions.

- *Drugs:* including marijuana legalization and the War on Drugs. Texas's long border with Mexico informs Perry's view on fighting drugs as a border issue.

- *Environment:* including pollution and EPA issues. Perry implemented a "flexible permitting" plan as Texas governor.

- *Technology and Infrastructure:* including high-tech Internet and privacy issues, as well as low-tech roads and bridges investment issues.

- *Healthcare:* including federal healthcare and ObamaCare issues; plus Medicare/Medicaid and state issues. Romney implemented a statewide plan while governor of Massachusetts, which his opponents call "RomneyCare." Texas under Perry has no such plan.

Mitt Romney
on Domestic Issues

Rick Perry
on Domestic Issues

Romney on same-sex marriage

MA Constitution, by John Adams, has no same-sex marriage

I've been in a state that has gay marriage, and I recognize that the consequences of gay marriage fall far beyond just the relationship between a man and a woman. They also relate to our kids and the right of religion to be practiced freely in a society.

The status of marriage, if it's allowed among the same sex individuals in one state is going to spread to the entire nation. And that's why it's important to have a national standard for marriage. And I'm committed to making sure that we reinforce the institution of marriage in this country by insisting that all states have a right to have marriage as defined as between a man and a woman; and we don't have unelected judges saying we're going to impose same-sex marriage where it was clearly not in their state constitution.

My state's constitution was written by John Adams. It isn't there. I've looked. The people need to speak on this issue and make sure that marriage is preserved as between a man and a woman.

Source: 2007 GOP primary debate in Orlando, Florida, Oct. 21, 2007

Perry on same-sex marriage

Gay marriage is not protected, but judges will declare it so

In 2003, the Supreme Court heard the case of two homosexual men who had been arrested and convicted under a Texas law that prohibited the act of sodomy. Reversing its decision from 17 years earlier (upholding a Georgia ban), the Court found a right to homosexual sodomy. Justice Kennedy explained why by digging back into a special concurrence from the "Casey" decision upholding abortion when he wrote, "At the heart of liberty is the right to define one's own concept of existence, of meaning, of the universe, and of the mystery of human life."

I don't even know what that means, but it certainly has nothing to do with the Constitution or the law.

The real concern lies with the direction the Court clearly wishes to take the nation yet refuses to admit. Gay marriage will soon be the policy of the United States, irrespective of federalism the Constitution, or the wishes of the American people. Not because it actually is protected in the Constitution, but because judges will declare it so.

Source: Fed Up!, by Gov. Rick Perry, pp. 109–110, Nov. 15, 2010

NOTE: The "Casey" decision refers to the 1992 Supreme Court case, *Planned Parenthood of Southeastern Pennsylvania v. Casey*. The Supreme Court upheld the 1973 *Roe v. Wade* decision that established the right to an abortion, but allowed restrictions on abortion. The Court cited the right to privacy, as well as *"stare decisis,"* which means that a longstanding legal precedent should not be overturned without a good reason.

Romney on gays in the Boy Scouts

1994: Gays OK in Boy Scouts

Here's a brief review of Romney's public record on gay rights in his 1994 campaign against Senator Edward Kennedy.

- Supports federal legislation to prohibit discrimination in the workplace against homosexuals.

- Supports President Clinton's "don't ask/don't tell" policy for gays in the military.

- Says homosexuals should be allowed to participate in the Boy Scouts

- Endorsed by the Massachusetts Log Cabin Republicans.

Source: Mitt Romney: The Man, His Values, and His Vision, pp. 58-59, Aug. 31, 2007

NOTE: The Clinton administration in 1993 enacted a "don't ask/don't tell" (DADT) policy for gays in the military. Under the DADT rules, gays could be discharged from the military for homosexual contact and for stating their sexual orientation, but the military is not allowed to ask them their orientation. The DADT policy was repealed in 2010; since then, gays may serve openly in the military.

Perry on gays in the Boy Scouts

Homosexuals are inappropriate role model for adolescent boys

BSA units do not routinely ask a prospective adult leader about his (or her) sex life. The organization takes the position that this subject is a private matter and certainly not part of any Scout program. In the Scout Oath, the boy promises to be "morally straight." The Boy Scout Handbook says that to be "morally straight" is "to be a person of strong character. The BSA's position is that a homosexual who makes his sex life a public matter is not an appropriate role model of the Scout Oath and Law for adolescent boys. I do not believe the teaching of sexual preference fits within the parameters of Scouting's mission. The defining characteristics of homosexuality and heterosexuality is sex. Scouting is not intended to advance a discussion about sexual activity, whether of the heterosexual or homosexual form. You will find few parents of Scouts concerned about the homosexual scoutmaster whose sexuality is not disclosed as long as sexuality in no way enters into the scout-scoutmaster relationship.

Source: On My Honor, by Gov. Rick Perry, p. 69, Feb. 12, 2008

Romney on mandatory sentencing

One Strike, You're Ours: lifetime GPS tracking

Governor Romney announced that he would propose a "One Strike, You're Ours" law for those convicted of preying on children using the Internet. Massachusetts Republican District Attorneys and Sheriffs support Governor Romney's proposal for stiff mandatory jail time to be followed by lifetime tracking by Global Positioning Satellite (GPS) for first-time offenders: "As Governor of Massachusetts, Mitt Romney was a strong defender of children. He led the effort to put photos of the state's most dangerous sex offenders on the Internet and made it easier to extend civil commitments for sex offenders. As a candidate for president, Governor Romney is once again demonstrating strong leadership in protecting our children. His 'One Strike, You're Ours' law is an important initiative to strengthen law enforcement and protect America's sons and daughters. We are proud to stand alongside Governor Romney in his campaign for our nation's highest office."

Source: press release, "Law Enforcement Officials," July 21, 2007

NOTE: "Three Strikes" laws mandate that criminal offenders are sentenced to life imprisonment upon their third criminal conviction. The term refers to the baseball rule, "Three Strikes and You're Out." Romney's term "One Strike" is intended to be a stricter version of Three Strikes.

Perry on mandatory sentencing

Life without parole for certain repeat sex offenders

The pursuit of true stability and security also requires us to maintain law and order and keep our citizens safe. Last fall, I proposed legislation targeting sex offenders, to better protect our citizens. We should empower prosecutors to seek life without parole for certain repeat sex offenders, and requiring active GPS monitoring of high risk offenders for three years after they've done their time and been released by the Texas Department of Criminal Justice.

Source: 2011 Texas State of the State address, Feb. 8, 2011

Tough and smart: jail sexual offenders; release nonviolent

When it comes to criminal justice, I believe we can take an approach to crime that is both tough and smart. I agree with our Lieutenant Governor that sexual offenders who harm our children must face tougher penalties. At the same time, there are thousands of nonviolent offenders in the system whose future we cannot ignore. Let's focus more resources on rehabilitating those offenders so we can ultimately spend less money locking them up again.

Source: 2007 Texas State of the State address, Feb. 6, 2007

Romney on capital punishment

Supports death penalty in heinous murders

Romney pushes for a death penalty law for murderers convicted of heinous first-degree homicides. "The ultimate penalty should be available in Massachusetts for criminals who commit the most egregious murders," Romney said.

Source: Campaign website, www.romney2002.com, "Issues," Sept. 17, 2002

Favored stricter sentencing and death penalty

- Supported death penalty

- Wanted to abolish parole, limit probation, and end furloughs and release programs for violent or repeat offenders

- Favored mandatory sentencing and three strikes and you're out

- Supported restrictions on plea bargaining

- His crime prevention efforts also focused on instilling family values.

Source: Boston Globe review of 1994 campaign issues, Mar. 21, 2002

Perry on capital punishment

Death penalty for aggravated rape

The people are forced to check their view of what should be an appropriate punishment with the Supreme Court case of *Kennedy v. Louisiana*, which involved a sentence of death for a man convicted of rape. This case demonstrates just how out of touch with America the Court truly is.

Patrick Kennedy was sentenced to death not just for rape, but for the rape of his 8-year-old stepdaughter. The little girl suffered massive trauma to her genital area. The injuries were so severe that she required emergency invasive surgery to attempt to repair the damage.

Kennedy refused a plea deal that would have taken the death penalty off the table. He was then convicted under a 1995 statute that provided for the death penalty for anyone convicted of raping a child under 12.

A jury of his peers sentenced him to death, and Kennedy appealed to the Supreme Court. Texas supported Louisiana. The Court ruled the law unconstitutional, citing the prohibition in the Eighth Amendment against cruel and unusual punishment.

Source: Fed Up!, by Gov. Rick Perry, pp. 99–100, Nov. 15, 2010

Romney on gun control

OK to ban lethal weapons that threaten police

Q: Are you still for the Brady Bill?

A: The Brady Bill has changed over time, and, of course, technology has changed over time. I would have supported the original assault weapon ban. I signed an assault weapon ban as Massachusetts governor because it provided for a relaxation of licensing requirements for gun owners in Massachusetts, which was a big plus. And so both the pro-gun and the anti-gun lobby came together with a bill, and I signed that. And if there is determined to be, from time to time, a weapon of such lethality that it poses a grave risk to our law enforcement personnel, that's something I would consider signing. There's nothing of that nature that's being proposed today in Washington. But I would look at weapons that pose extraordinary lethality.

We should check on the backgrounds of people who are trying to purchase guns. We also should keep weapons of unusual lethality from being on the street. And finally, we should go after people who use guns in the commission of crimes or illegally, but we should not interfere with the right of law-abiding citizens to own guns, for their own personal protection or hunting or any other lawful purpose. I support the work of the NRA. I'm a member of the NRA. But do we line up on every issue? No, we don't.

Source: Meet the Press: 2007 "Meet the Candidates" series, Dec. 16, 2007

Perry on gun control

Individual right to keep and bear arms

Look at state involvement in our individual right to keep and bear arms. At least 40 states have laws on the books allowing their citizens to carry a weapon in some form or another, and many of those have reciprocity agreements with other states. Recently a number of states have also begun pushing back against what they perceive as the overreach of federal law against their citizens through the Commerce Clause. For example, Montana and Tennessee are getting tired of federal gun laws that reach down into areas traditionally left to the states, so they passed laws to protect from federal reach firearms that are manufactured and sold entirely within the state.

The natural question arises, How, then, do the laws get enforced? The Supreme Court made crystal clear in the *US v. Printz* case, involving the enforcement of temporary provisions of the Brady Handgun Violence Prevention Act, that the federal government cannot commandeer state authorities to carry out federal law.

Source: Fed Up!, by Gov. Rick Perry, pp. 163–165, Nov. 15, 2010

NOTE: The Supreme Court ruled on the issue of "individual rights," in the 2008 case called *District of Columbia v. Heller*, that the Second Amendment does define an individual right to gun ownership, as opposed to a "collective right" for a state-run and state-armed National Guard.

Romney on the War on Drugs

Combat the ruthless narco-terrorists in Colombia

On the 197th anniversary of Colombia's independence, we honor the many contributions that Colombian-Americans have made to our country. We also express our abiding solidarity with the Colombian people, who are fighting to secure their country's future from leftist guerrillas and narco-terrorists who have thrived on terror, violence, and corruption for too many years.

A safe and prosperous Western Hemisphere requires a strong and democratic Colombia. The US must continue to provide strong support for Colombia's efforts to combat the ruthless narco-terrorists that operate there. Our partnership with Colombia contributes to our security and our quality of life—sowing stability in a critical region and helping keep deadly drugs off our streets. We can and must consolidate the gains we have made in Colombia by strengthening the economic ties between our countries. The US Congress must treat this vital ally with the respect Colombia deserves and move forward now with the free trade agreement.

Source: press release, "Colombia Independence Day," July 20, 2007

NOTE: The US "partnership with Colombia" refers to the US policy called "Plan Colombia." Under Plan Colombia, the US provides international aid to the government of Colombia in exchange for aerial spraying of cocaine crops and other anti-narcotic activities.

Perry on the War on Drugs

Drug trade causes soaring violence on southern border

President Obama is [doing] just enough to create the impression of some activity to address border security. He announced that he will send 1,200 National Guard troops to the border, as a temporary measure, until an additional 1,000 Border Patrol agents are on the job. This has generated headlines—and I suppose it is better than the alternative of no additional troops or officers—but it is really a drop in the bucket. Consider that of those 1,200 troops, only 286 were assigned to Texas. The southern border of the United States stretches 1,954 miles, and 1,255 of them are in Texas. We have 60 percent of the border, yet less than 25 percent of the resources were given to Texas to deal with it. In the face of the soaring violence infesting our border communities as a result of the drug trade, this paltry effort is simply inviting more problems.

Source: Fed Up!, by Gov. Rick Perry, p. 124, Nov. 15, 2010

Romney on medical marijuana

Opposes legalization of recreational or medical marijuana

The former Massachusetts governor opposes the legalization of recreational or medical marijuana, although he endorsed the use of synthetic pot. In his most recent book, *No Apology*, he attributes the legalization movement to "the passion and zeal of those members of the pleasure-seeking generation that never grew up."

Source: Tim Murphy in Mother Jones magazine, Apr. 20, 2011

NOTE: As of 2012, medical marijuana is legal or partially legal in the District of Columbia and 17 states: Alaska, Arizona, California, Colorado, Hawaii, Maine, Maryland, Michigan, Montana, Nevada, New Jersey, New Mexico, Oregon, Rhode Island, Vermont, Virginia, and Washington. Medical marijuana is also legal in numerous foreign countries. Medical marijuana alleviates symptoms associated with glaucoma, cancer, HIV/AIDS, and numerous mental diseases.

Perry on medical marijuana

Medical marijuana OK for California, but not Texas

[On states' rights], there's a movement I disagree with, while appreciating the desire of Californians to decide for themselves—this is the issue of marijuana consumption. A few years ago Californians legalized the limited medicinal use of marijuana, but the Supreme Court struck this law down in *Gonzalez v. Raich*, claiming that the federal government has the power to regulate activity that would have a substantial effect on interstate commerce. Now, I am not sure the people of Texas would want to go down this road.

Keeping in mind that in 2008, less than 1% of the 847,000 marijuana-related arrests were carried out by federal law enforcement, it sure seems unlikely that there could be adequate resources at the federal level to actually tell Californians how to live their lives. In other words, Californians may well be telling the federal government to "bring it on," we'll handle this how we want to handle it.

Source: Fed Up!, by Gov. Rick Perry, pp. 164-165, Nov. 15, 2010

Romney on environment

Clean environment will be a campaign theme

Seizing on the momentum of his successful leadership of the Olympics in Salt Lake City, Romney revealed a campaign theme that relies heavily on his management and leadership experience.

"There have been too many left behind," Romney said after his announcement, in response to reporters' questions. "Our schools aren't solid enough; our environment has not been cleaned the way it could be. Our streets are not as safe as they could be. All these things could be made better in my view with the application of new leadership and sound management principles."

The millionaire venture capitalist said voters should not have trouble connecting with his candidacy. "Everything I've done over the last three years, I think, makes it clear that I'm very much connected with the people of our country and the people of our world," he said.

Source: Stephanie Ebbert, Boston Globe, p. B6, Mar. 20, 2002

Perry on environment

Stop declaring wildlife sanctuaries on water reservoirs

We are tired of environmental extremists entrenched in the federal bureaucracy undermining our regional water planning process. We support wildlife sanctuaries, but please stop declaring them on land local officials have identified as viable for water reservoirs.

In short our message to Washington is this: let Texans run Texas. I support legislation that establishes more than 20 reservoir sites in statute because securing viable water supplies is vital to the future of this state.

Source: 2007 Texas State of the State address, Feb. 6, 2007

Romney on pollution permits

States should be able to have their own emissions standards

Q: Schwarzenegger has proposed that California be allowed to implement much tougher environmental regulations on emission requirements than apply to the rest of the country. Do you side with the governor or with the Bush administration?

A: I side with states to be able to make their own regulations with regards to emissions within their own states. I side with states being able to make their own decisions, even if I don't always agree with the decisions they make.

Source: 2008 Republican debate at Reagan Library in Simi Valley, Jan. 30, 2008

Perry on pollution permits

Flexible permitting: cap emissions for entire facility

Obama's EPA doesn't care much for Texas's innovative flexible-permitting system, which establishes pollution caps for entire facilities rather than for each source (like a smokestack) within the facility. This flexible approach requires refineries and other businesses to contain their overall emissions, therefore satisfying the federal standards, but allows them the leeway to determine how best and most efficiently to do so. It was put in place under Democratic governor Ann Richards while Bill Clinton was president, and was never disapproved by the federal bureaucrats. In June 2010, the EPA broadened its takeover, invalidating all 122 flexible permits.

The EPA must have stepped in to stop a major pollution problem, right? Actually, Texas's commonsense system has been hugely successful in tackling air pollution. Over the past decade, Texas has achieved a 22% reduction in ozone and a 46% reduction in NOx emissions, outpacing the rest of the country, which achieved only a 27% reduction in NOx.

Source: Fed Up!, by Gov. Rick Perry, p. 89, Nov. 15, 2010

Romney on highway infrastructure

Invest in infrastructure from growing economy by lower taxes

Q: Do you want to raise taxes to fix more bridges? Or can we cut taxes to fix more bridges?

A: There's no question—if you really want to make some money in this country, really get some money so we can repair our infrastructure and build for the future, the biggest source of that is a growing American economy. If the economy is growing slowly, when tax revenues hardly move at all, and, boy, you better raise taxes to get more money for all the things you want to do. But if the economy is growing quickly, then we generate all sorts of new revenue. And the best way to keep the economy rolling is to keep our taxes down. Our bridges—let me tell you what we did in our state. We found that we had 500 bridges, roughly, that were deemed structurally deficient. And so we changed how we focused our money. Instead of spending it to build new projects—the bridge to nowhere, new trophies for congressmen—we instead said, "Fix it first." We have to reorient how we spend our money.

Source: 2007 GOP Iowa Straw Poll debate, Aug. 5, 2007

Perry on highway infrastructure

Trans-Texas corridor:
4000 miles of highway & utilities

One of the biggest objections Tea Party groups have with Perry is his support for the Trans-Texas Corridor—a plan that would have created more than 4,000 miles of superhighways, rails, and utility lines, cost more than $100 billion and required the taking of private property through eminent domain. The proposal was eliminated by the state Legislature this year.

Source: Alan Gomez in USA Today, "Tea Party," Aug. 8, 2011

Romney on technology education

To compete globally,
invest in education and technology

"We have to keep our markets open or we go the way of Russia and the Soviet Union, which is a collapse. And I recognize there are some people who will argue for protectionism because the short-term benefits sound pretty good, but long term you kill your economy, you kill the future. What you have to do in order to compete on a global basis long term is invest in education, invest in technology, reform our immigration laws to bring in more of the brains from around the world, eliminate the waste in our government. We have to use a lot less oil. These are the kinds of features you have to invest in; you have to change in order to make ourselves competitive long term."

Source: Mitt Romney: The Man, His Values, and His Vision, p. 114, Aug. 31, 2007

Perry on technology education

$40M for 5,500 students
in Texas Technology Grants

I am advocating that we set aside $40 million for a new Texas Technology Grant program. Texas produces 5,500 graduates a year in electrical engineering, engineering technology, and computer science while our economy produces 11,000 annual job openings in those fields. Let's invest in technology scholarships so that Texans are on the forefront of technology innovation, whether it is here at home, or in outer space.

Source: 2007 Texas State of the State address, Feb. 6, 2007

Romney on insurance mandates

Personal responsibility
instead of employer mandates

Q: What should we do with all the millions of people who are not insured?

A: Well, I actually got the job done. Working with people across the aisle, we said: Enough is enough. Look, the best kind of prevention you can have in healthcare is to have a doctor. And if someone doesn't have a doctor, doesn't have a clinic they can go to, doesn't have health insurance to be able to provide the prescription drugs they need, you can't be healthy. And you need to have health insurance for all of our citizens. And I found a way to do that without requiring raising taxes, without a government mandate, without a government takeover. When I said government mandate, I meant employer mandate. Instead, we have personal responsibility. We allowed individuals to buy their own policies. Those that couldn't afford them, we helped them buy their policies. And you know what? It cost us no more money to help people buy insurance policies that they could afford than it was costing us before, handing out free care.

Source: 2007 Republican primary debate on Univision, Dec. 9, 2007

Perry on insurance mandates

Wipe out ObamaCare; block-grant healthcare back to states

Q [to Romney]: Did the individual mandate work in Massachusetts?

ROMNEY: Our plan covered 8% of the people, the uninsured. ObamaCare is taking over 100% of the people.

Q [to Perry]: Massachusetts has nearly universal health insurance. It's first in the country. In Texas, about a quarter of the people don't have health insurance. That's 50th out of 50. It's pretty hard to defend dead last.

PERRY: Well, I'll tell you what the people in the state of Texas don't want: They don't want a healthcare plan like what Gov. Romney put in place in Massachusetts. What they would like to see is the federal government get out of their business. For instance, Medicaid needs to be block-granted back to the states so that innovation will come up with the best ways to deliver healthcare. I'll promise you, we'll deliver more healthcare to more people cheaper than what the federal government is mandating today with their strings-attached, here's-how-you-do-it, one-size-fits-all effort out of Washington, D.C.

Source: 2011 GOP debate in Simi Valley, CA, at the Reagan Library, Sept. 7, 2011

Romney on RomneyCare

RomneyCare intended as state plan; never as national model

PERRY [to Romney]: In your hard copy book, you said RomneyCare was exactly what the American people needed, to have that RomneyCare given to them as you had in Massachusetts. Then in your paperback, you took that line out.

ROMNEY: I actually wrote my book, and in my book I said no such thing. When I put my healthcare plan together, a Washington Post reporter asked, "Is this is a plan that if you were president you would put on the whole nation, have a whole nation adopt it?" I said, "Absolutely not. This is a state plan for a state, it is not a national plan." And it's fine for to you retreat from your own words in your own book [on Social Security's constitutionality], but please don't try and make me retreat from the words that I wrote in my book. I stand by what I wrote. I believe in what I did. And I believe that the people of this country can read my book and see exactly what it is.

Source: 2011 GOP Google debate in Orlando, FL, Sept. 22, 2011

Perry on RomneyCare

RomneyCare OK for Massachusetts, but not for Texas nor US

Q: Can a state like Massachusetts go ahead and pass healthcare reform, including mandates? Is that a good idea, if Massachusetts wants to do it?

PERRY: Well, that's what Gov. Romney wanted to do, so that's fine. But the fact of the matter is, that was the plan that President Obama has said himself was the model for ObamaCare. And I think any of us who know that that piece of legislation will draw a line between the doctor/patient relationship, that will cost untold billions of dollars, is not right for this country. And frankly, I don't think it was right for Massachusetts when you look at what it's costing the people of Massachusetts today. But at the end of the day, that was their call. So, from a just purely "states get to decide what they want to do," I agree with that. And in the state of Texas, we don't think that's the way we want to go.

Source: 2011 GOP Tea Party debate in Tampa, FL, Sept. 12, 2011

Romney on federal vs. state health laws

I stand by what I did in Massachusetts; but not ObamaCare

Q: Do you stand by what you did with the healthcare mandate in Massachusetts?

ROMNEY: Absolutely. I'm not running for governor. I'm running for president. And if I'm president, on day one I'll direct the secretary of Health and Human Services to grant a waiver from ObamaCare to all 50 states. It's bad law. I'll get rid of it.

PERRY: RomneyCare was the plan that President Obama has said himself was the model for ObamaCare.

ROMNEY: First, I'd be careful about trusting what President Obama says as to what the source was of his plan, number one. But number two, if you think what we did in Massachusetts and what President Obama did are the same, boy, take a closer look, because:

- Number one, he raised taxes $500 billion, and helped slow down the US economy by doing it. We didn't raise taxes.

- He cut Medicare by $500 billion.

- We dealt with the people in our state that were uninsured, some nine percent. His bill deals with 100 percent of the people.

- He puts in place a panel that ultimately is going to tell people what kind of care they're going to have. We didn't do anything like that.

- What the president did was simply wrong. It is the wrong course for America. It is not what we did in Massachusetts.

Source: 2011 GOP Tea Party debate in Tampa, FL, Sept. 12, 2011

Perry on federal vs. state health laws

States innovate on healthcare; feds are one-size-fits-all

Q: Compare your healthcare ideas and Gov. Romney's.

A: In the state of Texas, we passed the most sweeping tort reform in the nation in 2003. We also passed Healthy Texas, which expands the private sector insurance, and we've driven down the cost of insurance by 30%. But the real issue is how to get the flexibility on Medicaid so that the innovators can occur in the states. That's where you'll find the real innovation in healthcare. The way to deliver healthcare more efficiently, more effectively is to block-grant those dollars back to the state and keep this federal government that has this one-size-fits-all mentality from driving the thought process that we've seen that's destroyed healthcare in this country today.

Q: The Washington Post fact-checker noted that Texas has had 16 waivers for Medicaid. How can you say that the problem is that the federal government has not given Texas enough flexibility?

A: They haven't anywhere near given the states [enough flexibility]. I think what you should see is the block-granting, not having to go to Washington, D.C., and ask them "Mother, may I?" every time you come up with a concept or an idea. Block-granting back to the states, I'll guarantee you the governors and their innovators in their states will come up with ways to better deliver healthcare more efficiently, more effectively, more cost-efficiently. And that's what this country's looking for, is a president who understands that we have these 50 laboratories of innovation. Free up these states from Washington, D.C.'s one-size-fits-all.

Source: 2011 GOP debate at Dartmouth College, NH, Oct. 11, 2011

Romney vs. Perry on Economic Issues

Economic issues focus on the recession recovery and all fiscal matters, including the following topics:

- *Budget & Economy:* including deficit spending and all aspects of the federal budget. The 2012 presidential race takes place amid the Great Recession; while President Obama offers the most appealing target for Republicans, Romney and Perry need to demonstrate why they are the best choice for replacing Obama's economic policy.

- *Corporations:* including corporate taxation and corporate welfare. Romney served as executive in Bain Capital, while Perry has primarily served in public office.

- *Government Reform:* focusing on the size of the federal government, which Romney and Perry agree should be smaller.

- *Jobs:* including unemployment and union issues, but not the underlying economic sources of job growth and loss (that's covered in the economic issues section). Texas with Perry as governor gained jobs while the rest of the US lost jobs. Romney claims a similar positive history in Massachusetts, while the US was not in recession.

- *Social Security:* including the current Trust Fund and changes for the future. In the September 2011 debates, this issue provided strong exchanges between Gov. Romney and Gov. Perry, concerning Perry's questioning the program's constitutionality vs. Romney's promise for long-term stability.

- *Tax Reform:* including income taxes, tax rates, and bracket redistribution. Romney supports redistribution of the tax burden to help the middle class; Perry supports the more hard-line view of no new taxes on the wealthy.

Mitt Romney
on Economic Issues

Rick Perry
on Economic Issues

Romney on fiscal policy

Avoid recession with immediate middle-income tax cuts

Q: What would be your immediate first step that you would take regarding fears of a recession and some sort of economic stimulus package?

A: Well, immediately I'd go to try and get a reduction on taxes on middle-income Americans. Specifically I proposed having people who earn under $200,000 a year be allowed to save their money tax-free. It means no tax on interest, dividends, or capital gains. It keeps more money in their pockets. It also means that we have more capital going into the marketplace available for business startups as well as for homes.

Q: So for families earning under $200,000 a year, you'd recommend some sort of immediate tax cut, is that right?

A: That's exactly right. This is middle-income Americans. These are where 95% of Americans live, and get their tax rates down, allow them to save for the future, allow them to make investments in their homes, be able to save for college. The best thing we can do is keep money in the homes of the American people.

Source: CNN Late Edition: 2008 presidential series with Wolf Blitzer, Jan. 13, 2008

Perry on fiscal policy

Balance our budget without raising taxes

We just can't forget that dollars do far more to create jobs and prosperity in the people's hands, than they can in the government's. Taking more money away from Texas families and employers is not the answer to our challenges because they've already sacrificed plenty. Balancing our budget without raising taxes will certainly set a nice example for the rest of the nation, but we have a bigger motivation. Balancing our budget without raising taxes will keep us moving forward out of these tough economic times, creating more jobs and opportunity and leaving Texas more competitive than ever. Now, the mainstream media and big government interest groups are doing their best to convince us that we're facing a budget Armageddon. Texans don't believe it and they shouldn't because it's not true. Are we facing some tough choices? Of course, but we can overcome them by setting priorities, cutting bureaucracy, reducing spending, and focusing on what really matters to Texas families.

Source: 2011 Texas State of the State address, Feb. 8, 2011

Romney on small business

TARP should not be used for auto company bailouts

I know we didn't all agree on TARP. I believe that it was necessary to prevent a cascade of bank collapses. For free markets to work, there has to be a currency and a functioning financial system. But we can agree on this: TARP should not have been used to bail out GM, Chrysler, and the UAW. And this is personal for me, I want the US auto industry to succeed. But that can only happen if its excessive costs and burdens are restructured. The right answer for Detroit is this: Fix it first.

All of these measures are meant to confront the current economic peril. Properly guided, Washington could in fact speed the recovery. So far, some of the actions it has taken will help, and some will hurt. But we can be certain that the American economy will recover. The invisible hand of the market is more powerful than the lumbering machinery of government. The private sector—entrepreneurs and businesses large and small—will create the millions of jobs our country needs.

Source: Speech to 2009 Conservative Political Action Conference, Feb. 27, 2009

NOTE: "TARP" refers to the Troubled Asset Relief Program, President Bush's 2008 program to purchase assets from financial institutions to alleviate the subprime mortgage crisis. President Bush approved using $17 billion in TARP funds for GM and Chrysler beginning in 2008, with the loan contingent upon the two automakers following federal government restructuring of their companies. The purpose of the bailout was to avoid bankruptcy and a large surge in unemployment of auto workers.

Perry on small business

Reduce businesses' tax burden and regulatory climate

Q: How would you help incent small businesses to hire new employees and to confidently grow our business in this troublesome economic environment?

PERRY: What we have done in the state of Texas over the course of the last decade is to lower that tax burden on the small businessmen and -women, have a regulatory climate that is fair and predictable, and sweeping tort reform that we passed in 2003 that told personal injury trial lawyers, don't come to Texas, because you are not going to be suing our doctors frivolously.

That's the way you get the government off of the back of small businessmen and -women. And that's the way you free up those small business entrepreneurs, where they know that they can risk their capital and have a chance to have a return on investment.

If it will work in the state of Texas, it will work in Washington, D.C. And that's exactly what I'm going bring to Washington when I go there in January of 2013.

Source: 2011 GOP Google debate in Orlando, FL, Sept. 22, 2011

Romney on corporate regulation

Corporations are people

Campaigning in Iowa, Mitt Romney told a heckler, "Corporations are people, my friend"—words immediately seized upon by Democrats in what they termed as a possible defining statement by the presidential candidate.

Romney, speaking to a crowd at the Iowa State Fair, was being pressed about raising taxes to help cover entitlement spending. When one mentioned raising corporate tax rates, Romney responded by saying corporations were no different than people. The line earned him a sustained round of applause from the crowd.

But the Democratic National Committee fired off emails almost immediately after the remarks, as part of a continuing effort to frame the GOP frontrunner as an out-of-touch elitist, writing: "This is what Mitt Romney is going to run on?"

A small band of hecklers, positioned near the stage, continually quarreled with Romney about whether wealthy Americans should pay higher taxes. "There was a time in this country when we didn't attack people based on their success," Romney said.

Source: James Oliphant in the Los Angeles Times, Aug. 11, 2011

Perry on corporate regulation

Texas is the land of freedom from over-regulation

PAUL: I'm a taxpayer in Texas. My taxes have gone up. Our taxes have doubled since he's been in office. Our spending has gone up double. Our debt has gone up nearly triple. [Perry claimed job growth due to tax cuts] but how do you pay for a tax cut? I think that's the wrong principle, because when you give people their money back, it's their money.

PERRY: While I've been governor, we have cut taxes by $14 billion, 65 different pieces of legislation. You may not have seen them, Representative Paul, but the fact of the matter is, there are people coming to Texas for five years in a row, the number one destination. They're not coming because we're overtaxing them. They're coming to Texas because they know there's still a land of freedom in America, freedom from over-taxation, freedom from over-litigation and freedom from over-regulation, and it's called Texas. We need to do the same thing for America.

Source: 2011 GOP Tea Party debate in Tampa, FL, Sept. 12, 2011

Romney on government spending

The "Party of No" is OK
when it comes to spending

The president accuses us of being the party of no. It's as if he thinks that by saying no, it's by definition a bad thing. In fact, it's right and praiseworthy to say no to bad things. It's right to say no to cap-and-trade, no to Card Check, no to government healthcare, no to higher taxes.

Our party can never be a rubber stamp for rubber-stamp spending. But before we move away from this "No" epithet that the Democrats are fond of trying to apply to us, let's ask the Obama folks why they say no: no to a balanced budget, no to reforming entitlements, no to malpractice reform, no to missile defense in eastern Europe, no to tax cuts. You see, we conservatives don't have a corner on saying no. We're just the ones who say it when it's the right thing to say.

Source: Speech to 2010 Conservative Political Action Conference, Feb. 20, 2010

NOTE: "Cap-and-trade" refers to a carbon dioxide (CO_2) emissions policy where the amount of CO_2 is "capped" at a government-specified emission amount, and then the right to emit CO_2 is "traded" via emission permits. A similar program was used successfully to battle acid rain via sulfur dioxide emission permits trading on the Chicago Mercantile Exchange.

Perry on government spending

Route to success is lower taxes & smaller government

I am proud of what Texas has done in the face of the economic challenges that have gripped our nation in recent years. We know that the route to success is lower taxes, smaller government, and freedom for every individual, because we have seen it work. Our job growth at the end of 2009 and an unemployment rate that has stayed well below the national average.

Indeed, the Texas unemployment rate is the lowest among the nation's ten largest states, as is our state's level of debt. Texas was named the top exporting state in the country for the eighth straight year. That's what happens when you free up citizens to compete. And as a result, we were able to finish our last legislative session with a balanced budget, a tax cut for 40,000 small businesses, and over $8 billion set aside for our state's "rainy-day fund." In fact, Texas and Alaska are responsible for two-thirds of all state dollars set aside in reserve. A sad indictment on the rest of America, this is a source of pride for those of us in Austin.

Source: Fed Up!, by Gov. Rick Perry, pp. 9-10, Nov. 15, 2010

Romney on capping government spending

Cap how much government can spend
as a percentage of GDP

If you go back a few years to JFK's time, the government at all levels—federal, state, and local—was consuming about 27% of the US economy. Today it consumes about 37% of the US economy. It's on track to get to 40%. We cease at some point to be a free economy. And the idea of saying, we just want a little more, just give us some more tax revenue, we need that, that is the answer for America.

The answer is to cut federal spending. The answer is to cap how much the federal government can spend as a percentage of our economy and have a balanced budget amendment.

And the second part of the answer is to get our economy to grow, because the idea of just cutting and cutting and taxing more—I understand mathematically those things work, but nothing works as well as getting the economy going. Get Americans back to work. Get them paying taxes. Get corporations growing in America. And I'll tell you, these kinds of problems will disappear.

Source: 2011 GOP debate at Dartmouth College, NH, Oct. 11, 2011

Perry on capping government spending

Don't trade tax increases for spending cuts; Balanced Budget Amendment instead

Q: President Reagan asked, "Do we reduce deficits and interest rates by raising revenue from those who are not now paying their fair share, or do we accept bigger budget deficits?"

PERRY: President Reagan was willing to trade tax increases for reductions, and I don't think he ever saw those reductions, he just saw the tax increase. As a matter of fact, in his diary he made that statement that he's still looking around for those reductions. One of the reasons that Americans are so untrustworthy of what's going on in Washington is because they never see a cut in spending. They always hear the siren song, "if you'll allow us to raise taxes, then we'll make these reductions over here," when the fact of the matter is the issue is we need to have a balanced budget amendment to the United States Constitution. And the next president of the United States needs to spend his time passing a balanced budget amendment to the United States Constitution.

Source: 2011 GOP debate at Dartmouth College, NH, Oct. 11, 2011

Romney on growth of government

Liberals replace opportunity with dependency on government

America cannot long lead the nations if we fail the family at home. Liberals would replace opportunity with dependency on government largesse. They grow government and raise taxes to put more people on Medicaid, to take work requirements out of welfare, and to grow the ranks of those who pay no taxes at all. Dependency is death to initiative, risk-taking, and opportunity. It's time to stop the spread of government dependency and fight it like the poison it is. It's time for big ideas, not Big Brother.

Source: Speech at 2008 Republican National Convention, Sept. 4, 2008

Perry on growth of government

America is great; Washington is broken

Something is terribly wrong. There is a sense among Americans that the world we have always known is in danger of being turned upside down.

Now, do not misunderstand me. America is great. Our nation has done, and continues to do, more for the cause of freedom around the world than any nation in the history of man.

But America is in trouble, and the people know it. We sense that our way of life and, perhaps more importantly, our ability to decide how we shall live, is no longer in our control but in the control of an increasingly powerful and oppressive national government—a government run by people who simply do not share our values or our beliefs and blatantly ignore its limits.

In short, it is not America that is broken; it is Washington that is broken.

Source: Fed Up!, by Gov. Rick Perry, pp. 3-4, Nov. 15, 2010

Romney on job growth

Built long-term pipeline for MA jobs; so job growth is slow

Q: The Boston Globe said that job growth during your years in office was the third lowest of any state in the nation, and manufacturing employment declined more than 14%.

A: I'll take exception with the Boston Globe. Massachusetts is a high-tech state, and a capital goods state. And that's a sector of the economy that responds very slowly to turnarounds. And by about 2½ years into my administration, we were able to turn that job decline around and we started adding jobs.

Q: During the four years you were governor, jobs grew nationally by a rate of 5.5%, but in Massachusetts they grew by 0.5%, and that was the fourth-worst record.

A: I came into a state that had no pipeline, no sales force that called on companies and encouraged them to come into the state. There was no activity of any significance to bring jobs to the state. And we went to work, legislature and I, to try and change that. It took us a while to get all the incentives in place.

Source: 2008 Fox News interview: "Choosing the President" series, Jan. 20, 2008

Perry on job growth

We created 1M jobs in TX while US lost 2.5M

Q: You have touted your state's low taxes, the lack of regulation, and tough tort reform as the recipe for job growth in Texas, but no other state has more working at or below the minimum wage. Is that the kind of answer Americans are looking for?

A: Actually, what Americans are looking for is someone who can get this country working again. And we put the model in place in the state of Texas. When you look at what we have done over the last decade, we created 1 million jobs in the state of Texas. At the same time, America lost 2.5 million.

Q: But the counterargument is the number of low-wage jobs and that unemployment is better in over half the states than it is right now in Texas.

A: Well, the first part of that comment is incorrect, because 95% of all the jobs that we've created have been above minimum wage. So I'm proud of what we've done in the state of Texas. And for the White House or anyone else to be criticizing creation of jobs now in America, I think is a little bit hypocritical.

Source: 2011 GOP debate in Simi Valley, CA, at the Reagan Library, Sept. 7, 2011

Romney on job losses

FactCheck: No, fewer US unemployed than Canadians employed

Romney claimed there are more unemployed Americans than employed Canadians, but that's not true: "Today there are more men and women out of work in America than there are people working in Canada. And in January, Canada created more new jobs than we did."

Romney is right about the January unemployment numbers: the US added 36,000 jobs and Canada gained 69,000. But it's not true that there are more Americans who are unemployed than Canadians who are employed.

As of January, there were 13.9 million Americans out of work; and 17.2 million Canadians employed. During his CPAC speech, Romney said there were 15 million unemployed Americans. That's wrong, but even if it were correct, it would be less than the 17.2 million employed Canadians.

The Romney campaign pointed to the number of Americans who are underemployed—including those who are in part-time positions while still looking for full-time work. But Romney spoke of Americans "out of work," and those who are underemployed are not out of work.

Source: FactCheck.org on 2011 Conservative Political Action Conf., Feb. 15, 2011

Perry on job losses

FactCheck: Texas job growth is strong, but predated Perry

Perry says Texas accounted for 48% of jobs created after recession's end, in an interview with Glenn Beck.

We recognize that job-gain boasts can overreach. An example: Perry's 2009 claim that about 70% of the jobs created in the US from November 2007 through November 2008 were in Texas. That was based on statistics from the 14 states in which job gains outnumbered job losses, and disregarded any jobs created in the other 36 states.

Perry got his new figures from the Dallas Federal Reserve, which subtracted the number of Texas jobs in June 2009 (10,287,000) from the jobs as of April 2011 (10,524,000) and determining the 237,000 increase accounted for 48% of the 496,000 jobs gained nationally over that period.

However, the Texas economy has been roaring since 1990, long before Perry became governor, including phenomenal job growth.

The strength of the Texas economy, compared to many other states, isn't in dispute. However, there are many ways to slice and dice employment statistics. Mark Perry's statement "half true."

Source: FactCheck on 2011 Presidential primary by PolitiFact.com, June 14, 2011

Romney on fixing Social Security

Will try to fix Social Security
without raising taxes

Q: Will you do for Social Security what Reagan did in 1983?

A: I'm not going to raise taxes. Not only are you taking money away from their pocketbooks, you're also slowing down the economy. You slow down the economy, more people lose work. More people lose work, of course, you're having a lot of folks that really have their lives turned upside down. So, raising taxes is just something you don't want to do.

We're going to have to sit down with the Democrats and say, let's have a compromise on these three elements that could get us to bring Social Security into economic balance. You can have personal accounts where people can invest in something that does better than government bonds—with some portion of their Social Security.

We're going to have the initial benefit calculations for wealthier Americans calculated based on the Consumer Price Index rather than the wage index. That saves almost two-thirds of the shortfall. You can change the retirement age. You can push it out a little bit.

Source: 2008 GOP debate in Boca Raton, FL, Jan. 24, 2008

Perry on fixing Social Security

Trust Fund is an unsustainable Ponzi scheme

By far the most alarming problem is the looming implosion of New Deal and Great Society entitlement programs. The combined liabilities for Social Security and Medicare amount to $106 trillion.

Aren't you wondering about the Social Security Trust Fund you've heard so much about? The term "trust fund" leads one to believe that there is a stockpile of assets that can be drawn on to pay benefits. Not so. This trust fund is an elaborate illusion cooked up by government magicians. While it is true that there is an accumulated *accounting* surplus in this amount, the surplus exists only in a "bookkeeping sense."

Ponzi schemes are illegal in this country for a reason. They are fraudulent systems designed to take in a lot of money at the front and pay out none in the end. This unsustainable fiscal insanity is the true legacy of the New Deal. Deceptive accounting has hoodwinked the American public into thinking that Social Security is a retirement system and financially sound, when clearly it is not.

Source: Fed Up!, by Gov. Rick Perry, pp. 58-61, Nov. 15, 2010

Romney on Social Security recipients

Honor expectations of recipients, but take action for future

Romney says "statesmen" from both political parties should sit down and "say honestly: 'What can we do?'" to fix Social Security. Romney says the solution should "make sure that we honor the expectations" of those who are already getting Social Security and those who are about to get regular Social Security checks from the government, while at the same time ensuring the system will be solvent when the 30- and 40-year-olds of today reach retirement age.

Source: Radio Iowa, "Romney: reform," by O.Kay Henderson, Aug. 25, 2006

Perry on Social Security recipients

Solemn oath to people approaching retirement age

Q: Gov. Romney has been hammering you on your idea of turning Social Security back to the states, repeatedly.

PERRY: Well, let me just say first, for those people that are on Social Security today, for those people that are approaching Social Security, they don't have anything in the world to worry about. We have made a solemn oath to the people of this country that that Social Security program in place today will be there for them. It's not the first time that Mitt has been wrong. We never said that we were going to move this back to the states. What we said was, we ought to have as one of the options that state employees and the state retirees, they being able to go off of the current system, on to one that the states would operate themselves.

Q: Can you explain specifically how 50 separate Social Security systems are supposed to work?

PERRY: We never said that we were going to move this back to the states. What we said was, we ought to have as one of the options that state employees and the state retirees, they being able to go off of the current system, on to one that the states would operate themselves. As a matter of fact, in Massachusetts, Romney's home state, almost 96% of the people who are on that program, retirees and state people, are off of the Social Security program. So having that option out there to have the states—Louisiana does it, almost every state has their state employees and the retirees that are options to go off of Social Security. That's an option that we should have.

Source: 2011 GOP Google debate in Orlando, FL, Sept. 22, 2011

Romney on Social Security entitlements

Entitlements: focus on future
beyond next election

The entitlement liability can be rectified, and the first step is to create public awareness that pushes the issue to the front burner. That will require political leaders who believe that their next election is less important than their children's future to speak out. It will also require able and relentless investigative voices in the media to refuse to let candidates off the hook who do not confront this issue. Prior to the 2008 economic collapse, there was reason to be hopeful that these voices would emerge. But the turbulence and uncertainty surrounding the financial crisis may keep the entitlement emergency in the shadows, allowing politicians to continue to ignore it for a while longer. Unfortunately, President Obama has done nothing in his first year in office to call attention to this looming crisis or to advance any solutions.

Source: No Apology, by Mitt Romney, p. 156, Mar. 2, 2010

Perry on Social Security entitlements

Entitlement programs are $115 trillion; we must cut them

Q: What programs would you cut for long-term deficit reduction?

PERRY: It's the entitlement programs that are eating up this huge amount of money. When you look at Medicaid, Medicare, Social Security, and those unfunded liabilities, I think are over $115 trillion just in those three programs. Those are the places where you go where you have to make the really hard decisions in this country.

Q: What order are the cuts? You didn't mention defense spending.

PERRY: Well, obviously, Social Security is one of those where we either can go to a blended type of a program where we blend price and wages, and come up with a program, and can save billions of dollars there.

Source: 2011 CNBC GOP Primary debate in Rochester, MI, Nov. 9, 2011

Romney on tax relief

Lowering taxes, like Bush tax cuts, grows the economy

Q: Would you explain why your record on taxes is better than your competitors?

ROMNEY: Lowering taxes grows the economy. Lowering taxes helps build jobs and helps working families, and so I strongly have been of the view that one of the great lessons for Ronald Reagan was that lowering taxes helped build our economy. Senator McCain was one of two Republicans who voted against the Bush tax cuts. I believe the Bush tax cuts helped our economy grow and are one of the reasons that we're not in a recession today. Senator McCain continues to believe that that was the right vote to take, and I respect that that's his view. I just happen to disagree with it. As governor, I fought tirelessly to reduce taxes. We cut taxes some 19 times in our state, and we held down spending. I believe it's critical for our economy going forward that we lower taxes again and we do so for the middle class. I believe that will help stimulate our economy, and create the economic base for growth of our new jobs.

Source: 2008 Fox News New Hampshire Republican primary debate, Jan. 6, 2008

Perry on tax relief

Tax rebates & tax relief
instead of government spending

Today I have proposed a budget that invests in healthcare and higher education, a budget that cuts property taxes and eliminates accounting gimmicks, and that grows the Rainy Day Fund to more than $4 billion. Not only that, it expands upon the record property tax cut of last year by setting aside an additional $2.5 billion for tax relief.

One way to provide tax relief is in the form of a rebate. The appeal of a one-time rebate is that future legislatures don't have to find the money to sustain it. However, the will of the Legislature may be to provide rate relief instead. Either way is better than the alternative: which is having the money spent on more government.

And for the record, I don't believe cutting taxes is the same thing as spending. A spending cap is meant to stop runaway spending, not runaway tax relief.

Source: 2007 Texas State of the State address, Feb. 6, 2007

Romney on taxing the rich

Reduce the tax burden on middle-income families

I don't stay awake at night worrying about the taxes that rich people are paying. I'm concerned about the taxes that middle-class families are paying. They're under a lot of pressure. Gasoline's expensive. Home heating oil, particularly in the Northeast, is very difficult for folks. Healthcare costs are going through the roof. Education costs and higher education are overwhelming. And as a result, we need to reduce the burden on middle-income families in this country.

Source: 2007 Des Moines Register Republican Debate, Dec. 12, 2007

Perry on taxing the rich

Taxation is not the solution;
live within our means instead

Big government advocates and their friends in the mainstream media have marginalized the voices of those who protest as reactionary or lacking compassion.

Do you agree with them that the only solution to our challenges is more taxation? More borrowing? More spending? More central control? Me neither.

Over time, Washington has extended so-called "lifelines" to potential voting blocs lines that now bind the hands of state leaders and choke off individual liberties at every turn. As people of conscience, our challenge is to untie those knots that restrain us and return to the vision of the founders.

Americans want government that is leaner, more efficient, and less intrusive into their personal lives. They want government that will live within its means. Americans are obviously fed up with the so-called "progressive" movement that, long ago, set aside the people's interests in favor of expanding government and raising taxes while doing the bidding of labor unions and activist judges.

Source: Speech at 2011 Conservative Political Action Conference, Feb. 11, 2011

Romney vs. Perry on Social Issues

Social issues focus on matters that are based primarily on moral values, including the following topics:

- *Abortion:* including stem cells, partial birth, and state-level restrictions. This topic has always been the most viewed topic on our website www.OnTheIssues.org, so we explore all aspects of Romney's and Perry's positions.

- *Civil Rights:* including gay rights and minority rights. For the 2012 race, gay rights will dominate this category. While Romney was governor of Massachusetts, his state's supreme court passed the nation's first same-sex marriage law. Perry accordingly distrusts judges.

- *Education:* including college funding issues, school vouchers, and school prayer.

- *Families and Children:* including father's rights and family values.

- *Principles and Values:* including religious issues.

- *Welfare and Poverty:* including homelessness, welfare payments, and other poverty programs. Romney and Perry both focus on the underlying causes of poverty as well as the Opportunity Society as the means to exit poverty.

Mitt Romney on Social Issues

Rick Perry on Social Issues

Romney on Supreme Court and abortion

Firmly pro-life; including Court nominations

Q: [to Santorum]: You are staunchly pro-life. Gov. Romney used to support abortion rights until he changed his position on this a few years ago. Should this be an issue in this primary campaign?

SANTORUM: I think an issue should be looking at the authenticity of that candidate and looking at their record over time and what they fought for. You can look at my record. A lot of folks run for president as pro-life and then that issue gets shoved to the back burner. The issue of pro-life, and the dignity of people at the end of life, those issues will be top-priority issues for me to make sure that all life is respected and held with dignity.

ROMNEY: People have had a chance to look at my record and look what I've said. I believe people understand that I'm firmly pro-life. I will support justices who believe in following the Constitution and not legislating from the bench. And I believe in the sanctity of life from the very beginning until the very end.

Source: 2011 GOP primary debate in Manchester, NH, June 13, 2011

Perry on Supreme Court and abortion

Abortion only for rape, incest, or maternal health

Rick Perry said he believes abortion should be legal only in cases involving rape or incest or when carrying a pregnancy to term would threaten the woman's life.

Source: Associated Press on FoxNews.com, June 25, 2002

Romney on prenatal policy

Was effectively pro-choice
until cloning changed his opinion

Q: You were effectively pro-choice as governor?

A: About two years ago, when we were studying cloning in our state, I said, look, we have gone too far. It's a "brave new world" mentality that *Roe v. Wade* has given us, and I changed my mind. I took the same course that Ronald Reagan took, and I said I was wrong and changed my mind and said I'm pro-life. And I'm proud of that, and I won't apologize to anybody for becoming pro-life.

Q: Some people are going to see those changes of mind as awfully politically convenient.

A: When I ran for the first time, I said I was personally pro-life but that I would protect a woman's right to choose as the law existed. Two years ago, as a result of the debate we had, the conclusion I reached was that cloning and creating new embryos was wrong, and that we should, therefore, allow our state to become a pro-life state. I believe states should have the right to make this decision, and that's a position I indicated in an op-ed in the Boston Globe two years ago.

Source: 2007 GOP primary debate, at Reagan Library, May 3, 2007

Perry on prenatal policy

Protect the unborn
via sonogram requirement

We need to protect the unborn by fast-tracking the sonogram bill, so that women are fully, medically informed before they make the life-changing decision to terminate a pregnancy.

Source: 2011 Texas State of the State address, Feb. 8, 2011

Romney on legality of abortion

No punishment for women
who have partial birth abortions

Q: What would be the legal consequences to people who participated in illegal abortions?

A: They would be like the consequences associated with the bill relating to partial birth abortion, which does not punish the woman. No one I know of is calling for punishing the woman. In the case of a doctor, the kinds of penalties would be potentially losing a license or having some other kind of restriction. In the case of partial birth abortion, as I recall, the penalty is a possible prison term not to exceed two years. But generally the medical profession would immediately follow the law. That's not going to be an issue. And there would be a recognition that one's license was at risk if one violated the law.

Source: Meet the Press: "Meet the Candidates" series, Dec. 16, 2007

Perry on legality of abortion

The right to privacy is fictitious

The Court decided in 1963 that the people of Connecticut were unconstitutionally outlawing the sale of contraceptives, because—it imagined—in the "penumbras" of the Constitution there is a right to privacy that prohibits that policy. Penumbras? What total and complete nonsense. The justices made a policy and then made something up in the Constitution to effectuate it.

Eight years later the Court found that this "right to privacy" extends to the right of a woman to choose to terminate her pregnancy—a rather tepid euphemism for ending the life of the unborn baby. In what can only be described as an arrogant commitment to itself—an ode to its own legitimacy, if you will—the Court actually touted its self-given "authority to decide [the people's] constitutional cases and speak before all others for their constitutional ideals." I assume the Court would like us to say thank you, but I also assume that the 52 million or so unborn children who never had a shot at the American dream may beg to differ

Source: Fed Up!, by Gov. Rick Perry, pp. 107-108, Nov. 15, 2010

Romney on federal abortion laws

Would be delighted to sign federal ban on all abortions

Q: If hypothetically, *Roe v. Wade* was overturned, and the Congress passed a federal ban on all abortions and it came to your desk, would you sign it?

A: Let me say it. I'd be delighted to sign that bill. But that's not where we are. That's not where America is today. Where America is, is ready to overturn *Roe v. Wade* and return to the states that authority. But if the Congress got there, we had that kind of consensus in that country, terrific.

Source: 2007 GOP YouTube debate in St. Petersburg, FL, Nov. 28, 2007

Perry on federal abortion laws

Opposes federal abortion funding

Perry opposes the Christian Coalition survey question on funding abortion.

The Christian Coalition voter guide [is] one of the most powerful tools Christians have ever had to impact our society during elections. This simple tool has helped educate tens of millions of citizens across this nation as to where candidates for public office stand on key faith and family issues.

The CC survey summarizes candidate stances on the following topic: "Public funding of abortions, (such as govt. health benefits and Planned Parenthood)."

Source: Christian Coalition Survey, Aug. 11, 2010

Romney on stem-cell research

Stem-cell research lofty goals
don't justify destroying life

Romney adopted the "pro-life" label after his battle over stem-cell research. Ann Romney has multiple sclerosis. Romney, who not surprisingly cites the diagnosis of his wife's disease as one of the greatest blows of his life, is nevertheless alarmed by the aggressive program of embryonic stem-cell research consortiums. He has taken a stand against the Harvard Stem Cell Institute.

The Harvard Stem Cell Institute was seeking legal protection for an embryo production line for the purpose of creating and harvesting stem cells, and Romney refused his support. He said, "Lofty goals do not justify the creation of life for experimentation or destruction."

Romney's views would permit for research the use of embryos about to be destroyed by their parents; this puts him at odds with President Bush's more restrictive position. Romney has never supported state-funded research on embryonic stem cells, and is a believer in the efficacy of alternative methods of producing stem cells.

Source: A Mormon in the White House?, by Hugh Hewitt, pp. 111-114, Mar. 12, 2007

Perry on stem-cell research

Supports prohibiting
human embryonic stem-cell research

Perry supports the CC survey question on banning stem-cell research.

The Christian Coalition voter guide [is] one of the most powerful tools Christians have ever had to impact our society during elections. This simple tool has helped educate tens of millions of citizens across this nation as to where candidates for public office stand on key faith and family issues.

The CC survey summarizes candidate stances on the following topic: "Prohibiting human embryonic stem-cell research." [Supporting this statement means the candidate would ban such research; opposing it means the candidate would allow such research].

Source: Christian Coalition Survey, Aug. 11, 2010

Romney on school prayer

Schools can teach family values,
but not religion or prayer

Romney said he would support federal grants to schools to fund programs stressing the importance of economics and family values. He said that local school districts should have complete control over the programs, but that they could not endorse specific religious beliefs or prayer in schools. Among the possible programs could be teaching children to learn the importance of getting married before having children.

Source: Joe Battenfeld in Boston Herald, Aug. 1, 1994

Perry on school prayer

Supports voluntary prayer in public schools

Perry supports the CC survey question on school prayer

The Christian Coalition voter guide [is] one of the most powerful tools Christians have ever had to impact our society during elections. This simple tool has helped educate tens of millions of citizens across this nation as to where candidates for public office stand on key faith and family issues.

The CC survey summarizes candidate stances on the following topic: "Voluntary prayer in public schools and facilities"

Source: Christian Coalition Survey, Aug. 11, 2010

Romney on school choice

School choice over fat-cat CEOs of teachers' unions

Our conservative agenda strengthens our family in part by putting our schools on track to be the best in the world again, because great schools start with great teachers. We'll insist on hiring teachers from the top-third college graduates and we'll give better teachers better pay. School accountability, school choice, cyber schools will be priorities and we'll put parents and teachers back in charge of education, not fat-cat CEOs of the teachers' unions.

Source: Speech to 2010 Conservative Political Action Conference, Feb. 20, 2010

Perry on school choice

Choose from mix of public, charter & private schools

In 2026, I picture a nation filled with diverse people bound together by a commitment to liberty and a devotion to working hard to give their children a better life than their parents gave them.

I see a people who can pray in their schools as they wish and towns across America that can publicly celebrate Christmas, Hanukkah, or nothing at all.

I see an education system that is the envy of the world, controlled by parents and the people according to the beliefs of the communities in which they live. I see an energetic mix of public, charter, and private schools, delivering options so people can choose what is best for their children, rather than getting stuck because a too-powerful teachers' union or government bureaucrat tells them how they must learn. The result is an important balance of academic excellence, local values, and a firm understanding of our nation's core founding principles—all of which will carry our nation forward with new generations of American achievement.

Source: Fed Up!, by Gov. Rick Perry, pp. 170-172, Nov. 15, 2010

Romney on education vouchers

Supported means-tested vouchers
for public & private schools

• Pledged to vote to establish a means-tested school voucher program to allow students to attend the public or private school of their choice.

• Supported abolishing the federal Department of Education

• Favored keeping control of educational reform at the lowest level, closest to parents, teachers, and the community.

Source: Boston Globe review of 1994 campaign issues, Mar. 21, 2002

Perry on education vouchers

Start a pilot voucher program in Texas

The Supreme Court's ruling that government-funded vouchers can be used for tuition at religious schools may settle the question of constitutionality, but the fight will shift to state courts, in legal battles over state constitutional objections to voucher programs, and to state legislatures and the ballot box.

Texas is among several states expected to seriously consider creating a voucher program. Rick Perry, who said he supports the court's decision, said a voucher program could be developed next year in the Legislature, where similar bills have stalled before. "What it says is that parents have a place and role in the decision-making process about where their children go to school," he said. "It's about parental choice." Perry said he favors starting with a pilot program.

Source: Dallas Morning News, June 28, 2002

Romney on Department of Education

Changed from closing Education Dept. to supporting NCLB

Q: You have been criticized for changing your position on some issues. You say that it's a part of learning from experience. Can you point to an area in which your learning from experience led you to change to a position that is less popular with the Republican base?

A: Sure, quite a few, actually. One is No Child Left Behind. I've taken a position where, once upon a time, I said I wanted to eliminate the Department of Education. That was my position when I ran for Senate in 1994. That's very popular with the base. As I've been a governor and seen the impact that the federal government can have holding down the interest of the teachers' unions and instead putting the interests of the kids and the parents and the teachers first, I see that the Department of Education can actually make a difference. So I supported No Child Left Behind. I still do. I know there are a lot in my party that don't like it, but I like testing in our schools. I think it allows us to get better schools.

Source: 2007 Republican Debate in South Carolina, May 15, 2007

Perry on Department of Education

Do away with the Department of Education

Q: If a state continually fails to educate children adequately, does the federal government have an obligation to intervene?

A: No. If you believe in the Tenth Amendment, if you believe the people in that state can impact their legislators, they will do that. I think that's a situation we would not ever find ourselves in because by the time a school failed, the parents would have intervened and the legislature would have intervened. Our problem is that we've got a federal government that's intervening too much. I truly believe that the education of our children is a state and a local issue and the federal government needs to completely stay out of it.

Q: Would you be willing to get rid of federal assistance for school lunch? Pell grants? The GI Bill?

A: Absolutely. I think there's a better way to distribute those dollars. There may be some of those programs, like the GI Bill, that we leave in place, but the idea that the federal government needs to be taking billions of dollars from the states, and running it through the Department of Education, and then picking winners and losers—I don't agree with that at all. I'd do away with the Department of Education. I'd do away with it. I think that is a waste of time and a waste of money. The state is a substantially better place to educate our children.

Source: Fox News Mike Huckabee debate, Dec. 3, 2011

Romney on family values

Child development enhanced
by having a mother & father

The attack on faith and religion is no less relentless. Tolerance for pornography and sexual promiscuity, combined with the twisted incentives of government welfare programs have led to today's grim realities: 68% of African-American children are born out of wedlock; 45% of Hispanic children; 25% of white children. How much harder it is for these children to succeed in school and in life. A nation built on the principles of the Founding Fathers cannot long stand when its children are raised without fathers in the home.

The development of a child is enhanced by having a mother and father. Such a family is the ideal for the future of the child and for the strength of a nation. I wonder how it is that unelected judges, like some in my state of Massachusetts, are so unaware of this reality, so oblivious to the millennia of recorded history. It is time for the people of America to fortify marriage through Constitutional amendment, so that liberal judges cannot continue to attack it.

Source: Speeches to 2008 Conservative Political Action Conference, Feb. 7, 2008

Perry on family values

Free speech for "Coming Out Day" but not "Family Values"?

Recently in Oakland, California, a group of African-American Christian women who are city government employees formed the Good News Employee Association. They defined their group as a "forum for people of faith to express their views on the issues of the day, with respect for the Natural Family, Marriage, and Family Values." They posted their flier on an employee bulletin board after others had used the bulletin board to advertise "gay rights." They asked for formal approval to use the city's employee e-mail system and bulletin board regularly, but were denied on the grounds that their flier would "promote harassment based on sexual orientation."

Gay rights advocates employed by the city had used the communication system to promote "Happy Coming Out Day," but the city's bureaucratic overseers deemed the words "marriage" and "family values" unacceptable. This is but one example of efforts to limit free speech and to curb values that have been central to the American experience for many decades.

Source: On My Honor, by Gov. Rick Perry, pp. 155–156, Feb. 12, 2008

Romney on family strength

Strong military, strong economy, and strong families

A Boy Scout–led recitation of the Pledge of Allegiance and a prayer set the stage for former Massachusetts governor and presidential candidate Mitt Romney's family-values appearance in Cedar Rapids. Romney stressed his core beliefs in a strong military, a strong economy and strong families. "Family-oriented American people, God-fearing people who love liberty, who will sacrifice for liberty, that is the source of America's strength," said Romney. "It always has been, it always will be."

Source: Danny Valentine, Des Moines Register, June 17, 2007

To strengthen America, strengthen the American family

Romney said, "People, not government, are the source of America's strength. There is no place that is more important to the future strength of America than the American home. The work that goes on within the walls of a home is the most important work that is ever done in America. And if we want to strengthen America, we need to strengthen the American family." Romney's speech stressed family values, the need to cut off investments linked to Iran, and the belief in less government.

Source: Jason Spencer, Spartanburg Herald-Journal, Feb. 23, 2007

Perry on family strength

We gravitate to bad behavior
unless we revere authority

Most of the time, disobedience is a form of rebellion and a lack of respect for people in positions of authority. Reverence for authority starts in the home, where children learn the rewards and consequences of good behavior and bad. I am not talking about reviving an era of stern discipline, such as the use of the belt or the switch. I am referring to parents who allow their children to develop a sense of self so at odds with society that those children cannot conceive of respecting their peers, let alone people in positions of authority. We would all gravitate toward monstrous behavior if no one socialized us. It seems to be our "wild" nature to do so, and only proper nurturing can redirect us. The one thing every child does is have an innate desire to please his parents, perhaps just in the hope of getting attention. This desire must be put to good use. Establishing boundaries and norms and requiring children to stick to those rules to receive approval is essential.

Source: On My Honor, by Gov. Rick Perry, pp. 141-142, Feb. 12, 2008

Romney on religious independence

Freedom requires religion just as religion requires freedom

Freedom requires religion just as religion requires freedom. Freedom opens the windows of the soul so that man can discover his most profound beliefs and commune with God. Freedom and religion endure together, or perish alone.

Given our grand tradition of religious tolerance and liberty, some wonder whether there are any questions regarding an aspiring candidate's religion that are appropriate. I believe there are.

Source: Speech "Faith in America" at Bush Presidential Library, Dec. 6, 2007

Perry on religious independence

Supreme Court shouldn't choose how & where we may pray

To whom may the people realistically appeal when the Court arrogantly chooses to hide behind the Constitution while it implements its own policy choices? No one.

That the Court makes policy can hardly be debated—and that many of these policy choices affect the citizen at the core of his personal conscience is equally beyond question. Consider that it is our courts that routinely decide, with little or no chance of further appeal, how and where we may and may not pray to God, when life begins, whether contraception must be allowed to be sold, whether and how we can celebrate religious holidays, what those other than man and woman must be allowed to marry, what level of discrimination may carried out (in the name of ending discrimination), whether a state must allow women to attend an all-male military academy, who may be executed and whether we may execute criminals at all, and generally any issue involving social preference, morality, and our collective concept of right and wrong.

Source: Fed Up!, by Gov. Rick Perry, p. 96, Nov. 15, 2010

Romney on religious freedom

Freedom requires religion in society, not in individuals

Q: You said in your speech on faith, "Freedom requires religion just as religion requires freedom." Can you have freedom without organized religion?

A: Well, I was paraphrasing and underlining a quote from John Adams, who said that our constitutional form of government in this nation would require morality and freedom to be able to survive. We believe, as a nation, that God gave the individual certain inalienable rights. That's not a constitutional guarantee, that's not a policy guarantee, it's a guarantee from our creator.

Q: Can you be a moral person and be an atheist?

A: Oh, of course.

Q: So freedom doesn't require religion?

A: Our constitutional form of government and this American experiment requires morality, which in turn required religion. Yet, of course, on an individual basis, you have many individuals of great morality that don't have any particular faith.

Q: If a qualified person for the Supreme Court happened to be an atheist, would that prevent you from appointing them?

A: Of course not. You look at individuals based upon their skills and their ability, their values, their intelligence. And there are many who are agnostic or atheist or who have very different beliefs than I do, and you evaluate them based on their skills. But I myself am a person of faith and respect the sense of the common bond of humanity that comes from that fundamental belief.

Source: Meet the Press: "Meet the Candidates" series, Dec. 16, 2007

Perry on religious freedom

It's about freedom *of* religion,
not freedom *from* religion

The ACLU and like-minded liberals would have us believe that the Establishment Clause equates to freedom *from* religion rather than freedom *of* religion. Instead of a reasonable interpretation of the Constitution in a pluralistic society that protects our citizens from a state-sponsored religion being forced upon them, they want to take a more drastic step, which is to whitewash the public square and our public dialogue of any reference to God. Their view is that if one citizen believes there is no God, they must be protected from public references to an Almighty Creator. In an effort to protect a minority view, they go so far as to maintain the position that an atheist, or a non-Christian, cannot be exposed to the majority of religious viewpoints in America without unduly being indoctrinated. What about believing enough in your fellow men and woman to acknowledge that maybe they can think for themselves? What about the educational value inherent in Christian children being exposed to a menorah?

Source: On My Honor, by Gov. Rick Perry, p. 87, Feb. 12, 2008

Romney on religious faith

Americans want person of faith as president, whatever brand

One by one the other presidential campaigns have committed "accidental" attacks on Romney's religion. The presidential candidates were all quick to apologize for the actions of their campaign workers. In each case the candidates expressed regret and disappointment as they disavowed any attacks on religion. All stressed that they disavowed any attacks on religion. All stressed that they wanted to run a clean campaign that would not tolerate bigotry.

Gov. Romney accepted the apologies, saying, "Clearly, any derogatory comments about anyone's faith—those comments are troubling. The fact they keep on coming up is even more troubling."

It's not all negative, however. At an early campaign stop a man in the audience challenged Romney directly, telling him that he would surely go to hell. The crowd groaned, then booed the man. Romney responded with what has become his signature comment on religion. "I believe Americans want a person of faith to lead the country. It doesn't matter what brand."

Source: Mitt Romney: The Man, His Values, and His Vision, pp. 93-95, Aug. 31, 2007

Perry on religious faith

Secular humanism emanates out of man's sin of pride

I believe secular humanism emanates out of man's great downfall: the sin of pride. To put God on the throne of our lives, to surrender to a Higher Being in complete submission, in the secular humanist's mind, is to surrender credit for the accomplishment of one's life. It is essential to say, "I am not so great because everything I have ever accomplished is a gift from God." To some this is not an appealing notion. Yet, where does our capacity to think, dream and emotionally connect come from? It is a gift present within our DNA. This, by the way, is true even if there is no God (a notion I dispute) because our every gift emanates from the unique combination of the genes inherited from our parents.

The life of the secular humanist has a depressing end. Regardless of how great they may consider their accomplishments in life, or how much money they make, it is still the case that they have lived their life for a philosophy that elevates self instead of a worldview that elevates the Creator.

Source: On My Honor, by Gov. Rick Perry, pp. 180-181, Feb. 12, 2008

Romney on homelessness vs. dependency

Opportunity is in our DNA; dependency is death to initiative

What is it about American culture that has led us to become the most powerful nation in the history of the world? We believe in hard work and education. We love opportunity: almost all of us are immigrants or descendants of immigrants who came here for opportunity—opportunity is in our DNA. Americans love God, and those who don't have faith, typically believe in something greater than themselves. The values and beliefs of the free American people are the source of our nation's strength and they always will be.

The threat to our culture comes from within. The 1960s welfare programs created a culture of poverty. Some think we won that battle when we reformed welfare, but the liberals haven't given up. At every turn, they try to substitute government largesse for individual responsibility. Dependency is death to initiative, risk-taking and opportunity. Dependency is a culture-killing drug. We have got to fight it like the poison it is.

Source: Speeches to 2008 Conservative Political Action Conference, Feb. 7, 2008

Perry on homelessness vs. dependency

Many homeless chose their lifestyle; take a hard approach

When Los Angeles passed an ordinance prohibiting people from camping out on city streets and sidewalks throughout the day, the ACLU sued; the ordinance was ruled unconstitutional. Recognizing that some people suddenly find themselves homeless because of tragic, unanticipated circumstances, I would not say that all homeless people are voluntarily in their predicament. Many homeless have chosen their lifestyle—not as a conscious lifestyle choice made in prior years of sobriety but through a series of decisions that not only led to their homelessness, but also perpetuate it. They choose to drink, they choose to get high, they choose to engage in a life or crime, and often they choose to do it all on the streets instead of in shelters where there is strict enforcement of prohibitions on such behavior. The homeless need help. But the help they need is to make some of their behavior more difficult to engage in. If you take a hard approach to blight, then you create a disincentive for continuing blight

Source: On My Honor, by Gov. Rick Perry, pp. 127-128, Feb. 12, 2008

Romney vs. Perry on International Issues

International issues focus on foreign relations and anything involving foreign nations, including the following topics:

- *Energy and Oil:* including global warming, domestic drilling, and alternative energy sources. Perry's Texas is a major oil-producing state, but also near the 2010 BP oil spill in the Gulf of Mexico.

- *Free Trade:* including NAFTA (the North American Free Trade Agreement) and other bilateral agreements, plus opinions on the trade organizations like the WTO (World Trade Organization).

- *Immigration:* including border security; the border fence; and dealing with the current 12 million illegal immigrants in the US. Perry's border state of Texas requires that he deal with the issue personally as governor; his policy of in-state tuition for illegal immigrants' children was a major focus of the September 2011 primary debates.

- *Foreign Policy:* focusing on general policy outside of defense policy.

- *Homeland Security:* this category concerns defense policy, not war policy. This category includes defense spending issues; and defense strategy goals.

- *War and Peace:* including the current ongoing wars in Iraq and Afghanistan, plus the 2011 military action in Libya .

Mitt Romney
on International Issues

Rick Perry
on International Issues

Romney on energy efficient cars

$20 billion package for energy research & new car technology

Q: You pledged to offer a $20 billion package to help out the auto industry with energy research and new technology. One conservative columnist wrote, "Is that what a Republican should do, bail out a private industry?" Are you going to offer billions of taxpayer dollars to every industry that's in trouble in this country?

A: We spend about $4 billion a year right now on energy research to try and help us become less energy dependent on foreign sources. And I think over the coming years we need to increase our investment to become energy independent from about $4 billion a year to about $20 billion a year. Obviously, that has got to grow gradually because there are not a lot of places now that do the kind of research we need to do to get ourselves energy independent. But that's not just to bail out the automobile industry. That's not what I have in mind. I'm not looking for a bailout at all. Instead, it's saying that where we invest, we tend to do very well.

Source: 2008 Fox News interview: "Choosing the President" series, Jan. 20, 2008

Perry on energy efficient cars

$5,000 incentive for
plug-in hybrid electric vehicles

When we combine lower utility taxes with increased, diversified production, we will preserve our role as the nation's energy leader. Unfortunately, our strength in petrochemical production and refining makes us a big target on the radar of an increasingly activist EPA, whose one-size-fits-all approaches could severely harm our energy sector; an agency whose potential to harm our state with punitive actions will only increase in the months and years to come.

Rather than wait for more mandates and punishments for environmental non-attainment, let's continue encouraging innovation. I support giving Texans in the non-attainment areas of our state a $5,000 incentive towards a purchase of plug-in hybrid electric vehicles, using the funds Texans have already paid to reduce emissions, while providing a unique way to store wind energy. This will keep Texas competitive in an emerging technology and take advantage of an energy portfolio that grows deeper and more diverse every day.

Source: 2009 Texas State of the State address, Jan. 27, 2009

Romney on climate costs

Exporting carbon emissions to China
hurts US and planet

On global warming: "I want to make sure we don't do something which costs hundreds of billions of dollars in this country and makes us less competitive with China and India. If carbon-emitting manufacturing moves to other countries, we've done nothing for the planet and we've hurt ourselves immeasurably.

Source: Mitt Romney: The Man, His Values, and His Vision, p. 113, Aug. 31, 2007

Perry on climate costs

Don't put economy in jeopardy
based on unsettled science

Q: You said scientists are coming forward to question the idea that human activity is behind climate change.

PERRY: The science is not settled on this. The idea that we would put Americans' economy in jeopardy based on scientific theory that's not settled yet, to me, is just nonsense. I mean, Galileo got outvoted for a spell. But asking us to cut back in areas that would have monstrous economic impact on this country is not good economics and I will suggest to you is not necessarily good science. Find out what the science truly is before you start putting the American economy in jeopardy.

Q: Are there specific theories that you've found especially compelling?

PERRY: Let me tell you what I find compelling, is what we've done in the state of Texas. Not by some scientist somewhere saying, "Here is what we think is happening out there." The science is not settled on whether or not the climate change is being impacted by man to the point where we're going to put America's economics in jeopardy.

Source: 2011 GOP debate in Simi Valley, CA, at the Reagan Library, Sept. 7, 2011

Romney on global warming

They don't call it "America warming" but "global warming"

When you put in place a new cap or a mandate, and particularly if you don't have any safety valve as to how much the cost of that cap might be, you would impose on the American people, if you do it unilaterally, without involving all the world, you'd impose on the American people a huge new effective tax: 20% on utilities, 50 cents a gallon for gasoline—that's according to the energy information agency—would be imposed on us. What happens if you do that? You put a big burden on energy in this country as the energy-intensive industries say, "We're going to move our new facilities from the US to China, where they don't have those agreements." You end up polluting and putting just as much CO_2 in the air because the big energy users go there. That's why these ideas make sense, but only on a global basis. They don't call it "America warming." They call it "global warming." That's why you've got to have a president that understands the real economy.

Source: 2008 Republican debate at Reagan Library in Simi Valley, Jan. 30, 2008

Perry on global warming

Manmade global warming: "It's-All-Our-Fault" theory

You can't have rational discussions with the left about nature versus nurture or global warming because they claim science has already weighed in. Yet, science reveals new discoveries all the time. Here we are again at a well-worn crossroads: The left advocates tolerance while crushing dissenting views.

When it comes to manmade global warming, many scientists who once advocated it is caused by human activity have abandoned that theory after closer study. Where are the stories on this growing *scientific* movement? Alas, many in the news media have already invested too much in a particular storyline, just as some scientists continue promoting It's-All-Our-Fault theory because their research grants are dependent on it. In 25 years, when this theory has been discarded alongside other ideas that didn't stand the test of time, perhaps there will be a one-day story announcing its demise. Then the left will be on to its next theory created to advance a particular political agenda.

Source: On My Honor, by Gov. Rick Perry, pp. 185-186, Feb. 12, 2008

Romney on nuclear energy

Develop energy technology like nuclear or liquefied coal

We face serious competitive challenges globally unless we become serious with getting prices of energy down. It's a great opportunity for America to develop technology to lead the world in energy efficiency as well as energy production. And whether it's nuclear or liquefied coal, where we sequester the CO_2, far more fuel-efficient automobiles. These are some of the incentives that have to be behind our policies with regards to our investments in new technologies like ethanol.

Source: 2007 Republican debate in Dearborn, MI, Oct. 9, 2007

Perry on nuclear energy

Use federal funds for nuclear cleanup, with state input

Perry signed the Southern Governors' Association resolution:

Whereas, in order to protect the health, safety, and welfare of our citizens by maintaining safe and clear strategies for the transportation, disposition, and environmental clean-up of the nation's nuclear materials, including nuclear weapons materials, at DOE nuclear energy and weapons complexes; now, therefore, be it

Resolved, that the Southern Governors' Association urges Congress and the President in any national energy policy:

- provide full funding for all of DOE's past and present commitments related to clean-up operations at DOE nuclear energy and weapons complexes and disposition plans for nuclear materials, including nuclear weapons materials;

- provide full funding for all state public health and environmental sampling and analysis activities at DOE nuclear energy and weapons complexes;

- and provide clear instruction to DOE that states' rights must be respected and that plans regarding DOE sites for processing of DOE research and weapons waste must be made in consultation with the various states concluding in mutually agreeable terms.

Source: Resolution of Southern Governor's Association on Energy Policy, Sept. 9, 2001

Romney on free trade

Renegotiate trade deals with China and other countries

I understand why jobs come and why jobs go. I've done business in over 20 countries around the world, and I understand how we can build more strength in our own economy and that's by investing in education, investing in technology and innovation, getting ourselves off of foreign oil, and making sure that the playing field we play on around the world is level. It's not right now. We're going to have to renegotiate deals with people like those in China that manipulate their currency to put their products in advantage over ours. We want to make sure that we do not have a circumstance where people close down their markets to our goods because we can compete anywhere in the world. One out of three agricultural acres is planted to go off-shore, so don't put up barriers to keep us from being able to trade. The US can compete anywhere in the world, and to remain a superpower, we must compete around the world.

Source: 2007 Des Moines Register Republican Debate, Dec. 12, 2007

Perry on free trade

Welcome market of united Europe and ever-growing China and India

I see an America where the innovation and hard work of the American people creates still more opportunities, jobs, and wealth. I see a nation that is not cowering to the prospect of a united Europe or an ever-growing China and India, but rather welcomes those markets and many others as opportunities for the entrepreneurial and industrious spirit of the American people. I see a world where free trade opens up more doors and where people embrace trade's benefit to both America and the rest of the world.

Source: Fed Up!, by Gov. Rick Perry, p. 172, Nov. 15, 2010

Romney on China policy

China doesn't want to have a trade war; so push hard

Q: Candidates have talked tough on China before—George W. Bush did it, Barack Obama did it—but once elected, the president takes a much more cautious approach.

A: They have been played like a fiddle by the Chinese. And the Chinese are smiling all the way to the bank, taking our currency and taking our jobs and taking a lot of our future. And I'm not willing to let that happen. We've got to call cheating for what it is.

Q: Isn't that risking a trade war?

A: Well, now, think about that. We buy this much stuff from China; they buy that much stuff from us. You think they want to have a trade war? This is a time when we're being hollowed out by China that is artificially holding down their prices. On day one, I will issue an executive order identifying China as a currency manipulator. We'll bring an action against them in front of the WTO for manipulating their currency. If you're not willing to stand up to China, you'll get run over by China. And that's what's happened for 20 years.

Source: 2011 GOP debate at Dartmouth College, NH, Oct. 11, 2011

Perry on China policy

Focus on bringing jobs back from China like we did in Texas

ROMNEY [on videotape]: I will label China as it is, a currency manipulator, and I will go after them for stealing our intellectual property, and they will recognize that if they cheat, there is a price to pay.

PERRY: What we need to be focused on in this country today is not whether or not we're going to have this policy or that policy. What we need to be focused on is how we get America working again. That's where we need to be focused. I can promise you that we do that and we'll create an environment in this country where the manufacturing will come back to this country.

We did it in Texas. We brought CHI Manufacturing, that had business in China, back to the state of Texas. You free up this country's entrepreneurs where they know that they can risk their capital and have a chance to have a return on investment and all of this conversation that we're having [on a trade war with China] becomes substantially less impactful

Source: 2011 GOP debate at Dartmouth College, NH, Oct. 11, 2011

Romney on border security

Priorities: secure border, employer verification, no amnesty

Three Immigration Priorities: "We're going to have to secure our border first. #2, put in place an employment verification system to make sure we're giving jobs only to those people who come legally. And #3, for the 12 million already here we can't allow them to have a special privilege of being able to stay here indefinitely."

No Amnesty: "Any legislation that allows illegal immigrants to stay in the country indefinitely, as the new Z-Visa does, is a form of amnesty."

Border Security Is Number 1: "There are three key rules we have to follow. One is we have to secure the border. Two is we have to have an employment verification system to know who's here legally and who's not here legally. That's only fair to the employers to know who is who. And then, finally, for those people that are here legally today, while it may be fine for them to apply for citizenship, they should do so in line with everyone else and should be given no advantage.

Source: Mitt Romney: The Man, His Values, and His Vision, pp. 111-112, Aug. 31, 2007

Perry on border security

Secure the Mexican border against drug cartels

Texas has a lot of unique features, including a 1,200 mile international border and a long history of strong relations with Mexico. The security of that border is one of Washington's essential roles yet they continue their record of abject failure in that area.

As a result, we continue to deal with violent Mexican drug cartels who work closely with transnational gangs on our side of the border operating with no regard for the law or respect for life.

The bad actors in Mexico are getting worse, and the risks to our citizens continue to rise along the border and in communities across this country where drugs continue to flow. We need 1,000 National Guard troops to support current law enforcement operations on our border until they can provide those 3,000 more border patrol agents. We also need Predator drones flying along the Texas-Mexico border providing real-time intel to our state and local operation centers.

Source: Speech at 2011 Conservative Political Action Conference, Feb. 11, 2011

Romney on illegal immigration

I like legal immigration; let business determine visas

Q: In 2008, you said you favored allowing American companies to hire more skilled foreign workers. With unemployment at 9.1%, are you still for importing more foreign labor?

A: Well, of course not. We're not looking to bring people in for jobs that can be done by Americans. But at the same time, we want to make sure that America welcomes the best and brightest in the world. If someone comes here and gets a PhD in physics, that's the person I'd like to staple a green card to their diploma, rather than saying to them to go home. I want the best and brightest to be metered into the country based upon the needs of our employment sector and create jobs by bringing technology and innovation that comes from people around the world. I like legal immigration I'd have the number of visas that we give to people here that come here legally, determined in part by the needs of our employment community. But we have to secure our border and crack down on those that bring folks here and hire here illegally.

Source: Iowa Straw Poll 2011 GOP debate in Ames, Iowa, Aug. 11, 2011

Perry on illegal immigration

Illegal immigration cost Texas $928M in one year

A 2006 report by the Texas comptroller's office estimated the budgetary impacts of illegal immigration in Texas. The report found that approximately 135,000 undocumented students in Texas public schools cost the state $957 million in just the 2004-2005 school year. The comptroller's report cited incarceration and uncompensated healthcare as the two largest costs associated with illegal immigrants to local government entities in Texas. These two items costs local government $1.44 billion over a one-year period.

Of course, those living in Texas illegally also provide income to the state because of increased economic activity, sales tax, and property taxes (either directly or through rent subsidizing the property owner). But adding the estimated revenues and costs to both the state and local governments, Texas taxpayers were out $928 million in 2005.

Source: Fed Up!, by Gov. Rick Perry, p. 121, Nov. 15, 2010

Romney on immigrant benefits

Turn off the magnet that attracts immigrants

I learned this when I was with border patrol agents in San Diego, and they said, look, they can always get a ladder to go over the fence. And people will always run to the country. The reason they come in such great numbers is because we've left the magnet on.

And I said, what do you mean, the magnet? And they said, when employers are willing to hire people who are here illegally, that's a magnet, and it draws them in. And sanctuary cities, giving tuition breaks to the kids of illegal aliens, employers that knowingly hire people who are here illegally. Those things also have to be stopped.

If we want to secure the border, we have to make sure we have a fence, determining where people are, enough agents to oversee it, and turn off that magnet. We can't talk about amnesty, we cannot give amnesty to those who have come here illegally.

We've got 4.7 million people waiting in line legally. Let those people come in first, and those that are here illegally, they shouldn't have a special deal.

Source: 2011 GOP debate in Simi Valley, CA, at the Reagan Library, Sept. 7, 2011

Perry on immigrant benefits

Free in-state tuition regardless of immigration status

SEN. RICK SANTORUM: Gov. Perry provided in-state tuition for illegal immigrants.

PERRY: If you've been in Texas for three years, if you're working towards your college degree, and if you are working and pursuing citizenship, you pay in-state tuition there. And the bottom line is it doesn't make any difference what the sound of your last name is. That is the American way. No matter how you got into that state, from the standpoint of your parents brought you there or what have you. I'm proud that we are having those individuals be contributing members of our society rather than telling them, you go be on the government dole.

Q: Is that basically the DREAM Act?

PERRY: I'm not for the DREAM Act that they are talking about in D.C.; that is amnesty. What we did in the state of Texas was clearly a states' right issue. We were clearly sending a message to young people, that we believe in you. That if you want to live in Texas, that we're going to allow you the opportunity to be contributing members.

Source: 2011 GOP Tea Party debate in Tampa, FL, Sept. 12, 2011

Romney on foreign policy

Unless US changes course,
we'll no longer be superpower

We face a new generation of challenges, challenges which threaten our prosperity, our security and our future. I am convinced that unless America changes course, we will become the France of the 21st century—still a great nation, but no longer the leader of the world, no longer the superpower. And to me, that is unthinkable.

America is unique in the history of the world. In the history of the world, whenever there has been conflict, the nation that wins takes land from the nation that loses. [The US] took no land. No land from Germany, no land from Japan, no land from Korea. America is unique in the sacrifice it has made for liberty, for itself and for freedom-loving people around the world. The best ally peace has ever known, and will ever know, is a strong America.

Source: Speeches to 2008 Conservative Political Action Conference, Feb. 7, 2008

Perry on foreign policy

America shouldn't be in the business of adventurism

Q: You recently said, "I do not believe that America should fall subject to a foreign policy of military adventurism." Do you think President Bush was too quick to launch military intervention without thinking through the risks?

PERRY: I was making a comment about a philosophy; I don't think America needs to be in the business of adventurism.

Q: You were making a philosophical comment, but it's hard to understand philosophy without understanding specifics. Where are some of the places where we've seen military adventurism?

PERRY: That was a philosophical statement that Americans don't want to see their young men and women going into foreign countries without a clear reason that American interests are at stake. And they want to see not only a clear entrance; they want to see a clear exit strategy, as well. We should never put our young men and women's lives at risk when American interests are not clearly defined by the president, and that's one of the problems this president is doing today.

Source: 2011 GOP debate in Simi Valley, CA, at the Reagan Library, Sep. 7, 2011

Romney on the War on Terror

To win the war on jihad,
we need friends in Muslim world

To win the war on jihad, we have to not only have a strong military of our own—and we need a stronger military—we also need to have strong friends around the world and help moderate Muslims reject the extreme. Because ultimately the only people who can finally defeat these radical Islamic jihadists are the Muslims themselves.

Source: 2007 GOP Iowa Straw Poll debate, Aug. 5, 2007

American resolve in Iraq counters jihad with fortitude

The jihadists' history with America justifies their confidence that we will abandon the fight. In 1983, jihadists attacked US marines in Lebanon—and we withdrew. Then again in 1993, jihadists attacked US marines in Somalia—and we withdrew. In 2000, jihadists audaciously attacked the USS *Cole*, killing 17 American sailors, but we did nothing.

With all this history as a backdrop for their lectures to the young, jihadists have become quite confident in the knowledge that, time and again, we have underestimated their threat, their capacity to kill, and their steadfast resolve. This is a lesson they pass on to the young radicals in the making. Only in recent years has American resolve in Iraq and Afghanistan provided a counterexample of Western fortitude in the face of jihadist attacks.

Source: No Apology, by Mitt Romney, p. 71, Mar. 2, 2010

Perry on the War on Terror

Iraq: combat terror on their turf, not ours

Many establishment Republicans in Washington want to blame their losses on the war in Iraq. I simply do not believe that is true. While Americans rightly have a watchful eye on the commitment of our courageous soldiers to the Middle East, and while many American still want to hear a clear articulation of our mission there, most Americans realize the need to combat terror on their turf, not ours.

Source: Fed Up!, by Gov. Rick Perry, p. 146, Nov. 15, 2010

Secure freedom for oppressed people in Iraq and Afghanistan

Today our soldiers in Iraq and Afghanistan are on patrol, securing freedom for oppressed people, guarding the tender shoots of a blooming democracy, working to eradicate an infestation of terrorism, so that it does not revisit our nation. We have come too far and sacrificed too much to simply walk away and allow the dark forces of oppression to regain control of these places that have been consecrated by the blood of our nation's best. Instead, we must lead boldly, focused on preserving order as we prepare people who once lived in bondage to defend their own freedom.

Source: Memorial Day speech to veteran's group, May 26, 2008

Romney on Guantánamo

Closing Guantánamo leaves America vulnerable to another 9/11

President Obama won the favor of liberal commentators by pledging what it calls reform in the treatment of terrorist detainees. He's also promised to close down Guantánamo, without giving the slightest indication of the next stop for the killers being held there now.

But here's the problem. That is the very kind of thinking that left America vulnerable to the attacks of September 11.

This is not a law enforcement problem. It is the gravest matter of national security, with thousands if not millions of lives in the balance. The jihadists are still at war with America. Our government has no greater duty than a vigilant defense, and no greater cause than victory for America and for freedom.

Gestures that communicate a lack of resolve only embolden America's adversaries. With Iran seeking nuclear weapons, with North Korea already nuclear and selling its technology to the Syrians, it is essential that we construct a missile defense, now.

Source: Speech to 2009 Conservative Political Action Conference, Feb. 27, 2009

Perry on Guantánamo

Unsettled policy on Guantánamo
signals weakness to enemies

Almost a full decade after the attacks of September 11, 2001, Washington still has not settled on a policy for detaining and, if necessary, prosecuting enemies captured in the War on Terror. President Obama naively campaigned as if terrorism should be handled as a law enforcement matter, and in November 2009 Attorney General Holder held a major press conference to announce that Guantánamo Bay would be shuttered and that 9/11 mastermind Khalid Sheikh Mohammed would face a civilian trial in Manhattan. Both plans have crumbled in the face of public and congressional opposition, and to this day the administration refuses to decide what to do. Washington's paralysis on the seminal issue of our time—dealing with terrorists whose mission is to kill as many American as possible—signals weakness to our enemies.

Source: Fed Up!, by Gov. Rick Perry, p. 132, Nov. 15, 2010

Romney on Afghanistan War

Stay in Afghanistan until our generals say to leave

Q: Osama bin Laden is dead. We've been in Afghanistan for ten years. Isn't it time to bring our combat troops home from Afghanistan?

ROMNEY: It's time for us to bring our troops home as soon as we possibly can, consistent with the word that comes to our generals that we can hand the country over to the Afghan military to defend themselves from the Taliban. I think we've learned some important lessons in our experience in Afghanistan. I want those troops to come home based upon not politics, not based upon economics, but instead based upon the conditions on the ground determined by the generals. But I also think we've learned that our troops shouldn't go off and try and fight a war of independence for another nation. Only the Afghanis can win Afghanistan's independence from the Taliban.

Q: Congressman Paul, do you agree with that decision?

PAUL: Not quite. I make the decisions. I tell the generals what to do. I'd bring them home as quickly as possible.

Source: 2011 GOP primary debate in Manchester, NH, June 13, 2011

Perry on Afghanistan War

Secure freedom for oppressed people
in Iraq and Afghanistan

Today our soldiers in Iraq and Afghanistan are on patrol, securing freedom for oppressed people, guarding the tender shoots of a blooming democracy, working to eradicate an infestation of terrorism, so that it does not revisit our nation. Media reports from the front lines are filled with stories of gloom, defeat, and failure, and talking heads, whose only experience with sand and heat are from the beaches of Martha's Vineyard, sound the cry to retreat, but those who serve on the front line tell a different story. Time and again, I speak to soldiers who have seen the positive impact of US efforts and tell of Iraqi communities responding to the rule of law. We have come too far and sacrificed too much to simply walk away and allow the dark forces of oppression to regain control of these places that have been consecrated by the blood of our nation's best. Instead, we must lead boldly, focused on preserving order as we prepare people who once lived in bondage to defend their own freedom.

Source: Memorial Day speech to veteran's group, May 26, 2008

Book Reviews

OnTheIssues excerpts political books and debates as the primary source of the materials in this book. Following are four book reviews, plus links online to additional books and debates cited in this book.

Book reviews:

Additional book excerpts online:

A Mormon in the White House?, by Hugh Hewitt (2007)
www.OnTheIssues.org/Mormon_White_House.htm
The Man, His Values & His Vision, by Turner & Field (2007)
www.OnTheIssues.org/Man_Values_Vision.htm

Additional debate and speech excerpts online:

State of the State Addresses, including Gov. Perry (2011)
www.OnTheIssues.org/2011_State.htm
CNBC GOP Primary debate in Rochester, MI (Nov. 2011)
www.OnTheIssues.org/2011_Your_Money_Your_Vote.htm
GOP debate at Dartmouth College, NH (Oct. 2011)
www.OnTheIssues.org/2011_GOP_Dartmouth.htm

Book Review: *No Apology:*

The Case for American Greatness
by Gov. Mitt Romney (March 2, 2010)

This book, published in 2010, outlines Mitt Romney's case against Obama for the 2012 election. Its title makes Romney's case that Obama is an apologist for America (pp. 24-33) whereas Romney would instead "proudly defend her." If the title sounds arrogant, that too is Romney's intent: he claims that Obama is too weak in missile defense (p. 18); in defense spending (p. 31); in the War on Terror (p. 64); and in just about everything.

While this book focuses heavily on foreign policy and military issues, Romney also makes the domestic case against Obama. Romney reinforces his conservative credentials against abortion (p. 265) and against gay marriage (p. 269), since those credentials need substantial reinforcement in the view of many hard-line conservatives (Romney ran against Ted Kennedy for the Massachusetts Senate seat in 1994 as a pro-gay, pro-choice Republican).

But mostly Romney focuses on healthcare. And mostly he focuses on how RomneyCare (the Massachusetts healthcare plan initiated by Romney as Governor) is not the same as ObamaCare (p. 176). Mostly Romney's opponents will focus on how ObamaCare is based heavily on RomneyCare: the 2012 Republican primary voters will have to decide which view prevails.

On the question of whether Romney is running in 2012, this book answers unambiguously "Yes." Romney never actually *says* that, of course. But candidates never do. The book's purpose is to establish Romney as sharing core conservative values, which he will need to win the primary election. And the book's other purpose is to establish Romney's line of attack against Obama, which he will need to win the general election. In summary, this book outlines Romney's campaign plans for 2012.

Book review written May 2011;

full excerpts available online at: www.ontheissues.org/No_Apology.htm

Book Review: *Turnaround:*
Crisis, Leadership, and the Olympic Games
by Gov. Mitt Romney (June 15, 2004)

This book is about Mitt Romney's experience as the chairman of the Salt Lake Organizing Committee (SLOC), which ran the Salt Lake City Winter Olympic Games in 2002. Some of Romney's comments in the book hail back to his time at Bain Capital, or forward to his time as Governor of Massachusetts. But mostly it's about SLOC, so most of our excerpts are about the principles and values he developed and/or describes from there.

Romney is widely credited with "turning around" the Olympics, after a series of scandals within SLOC involving corruption and bad financial planning. Romney overcame both problems, and pulled off a successful Olympics, which was viewed as having recovered the integrity of the Games, while also turning a profit.

Romney's performance in the Olympics was exemplary and outstandingly positive. However, he claims he never thought about the political implications of running the Olympics; and he claims he never considered running for Governor while at the Olympics. I don't believe that for one second. Romney ran for Senate against Ted Kennedy in the 1990s, and made a decent showing against the single most entrenched incumbent in the Senate. Everyone in Massachusetts politics, including myself, always assumed Romney would run for office again, and fully expected him to segue from the Olympics to a gubernatorial run. If Romney was surprised by that turn of events, he was the only one!

Romney, in effect, rode the coattails of his Olympic turnaround to victory in the Massachusetts gubernatorial election of 2002. There was no gap between the two—Romney flew back from Utah and immediately entered the gubernatorial race. Similarly, there was no gap after Romney retired from the Governor's position—he announced for President the day after the inauguration of Deval Patrick, his successor. So Romney is still, in effect, riding the coattails of the Olympics in the presidential race.

P.S. Full disclosure: I worked as a senior (paid) staffer for the Robert Reich for Governor campaign, which was a Democratic campaign in the primary when Romney was the only Republican candidate. After Reich's loss in the primary, I volunteered with the Shannon O'Brien campaign, which directly ran against Romney in the general election.

Book review written Feb. 2007;
full excerpts available online at: www.ontheissues.org/Turnaround.htm

Book Review: *Fed Up!*
Our Fight to Save America from Washington
by Gov. Rick Perry (Nov. 15, 2010)

Gov. Rick Perry is not very well-known nationally. But he is considered in the top tier of prospects for the 2012 Republican presidential nomination (or vide-presidential nomination). This book is Perry's statement on why that should be the case. Readers looking for intense partisanship or charismatic leadership won't find that in this book—there is no evidence here supporting why the pundits declared, breathlessly, in June 2011 that Perry would and should enter the GOP race as the nominee-apparent. Readers looking for straightforward conservative viewpoints *will* find them here—Perry is a straightforward conservative Governor from a straightforward conservative state.

Readers will *not* find citations to those straightforward conservative viewpoints in the pundits' exclamations about Perry's heir-apparent status. In June 2011, when preparing a Rick Perry presidential page, OnTheIssues.org found that the mainstream media pundits' analysis of Perry was utterly devoid of any issue content whatsoever. The pundits seem not to know, nor care, what Perry's issue stances are. Their argument seems to be, "Perry governs Texas. Bush governed Texas. Bush won. Therefore Perry can win." The first three statements are true, but have neither political connection nor logical connection to the fourth statement. We recommend ignoring the pundits and the mainstream press until they read this website and this book—by reading this webpage you will know more than they do!

Perry says he wrote this book because he believes "that America is great but also that America is in trouble—and heading for a cliff if we don't take immediate steps to change course." (p. xvii) Perry addresses the presidential speculation too: "Cynics will say that I decided to write this book because I seek higher office. They are wrong: I already have the best job in America." (p. xvii) This book would certainly serve as a presidential plan; but we'll know by the end of the summer, so we'll let readers decide rather than add to the pundits' breathless speculation.

The core of Perry's book is this: America needs change; voters are fed up with the current situation; the solution is to empower states rather than the federal government. (see pp. 5-7 on the "fed up" list from which this book derives its title; see pp. 26-33 on anti-federalism; and the double entendre of the title is "We're fed up with the feds being powered up compared to the states").

Perry addresses a potential problem with running for president on that platform: that slaveholders made the same argument to defend slavery in the Civil War. Somehow (pp. 33-34) Perry concludes that, if only states' rights held true, slavery would have ended: it was the federal Fugitive Slave Act that really ignited the Civil War. We'll let the Republican primary process debate Perry's odd view of history on that issue!

Book review written June 2011;
full excerpts available online at: www.ontheissues.org/Fed_Up.htm

Book Review: *On My Honor*
Why the American Values of the Boy Scouts Are Worth Fighting For
by Gov. Rick Perry (Feb. 12, 2008)

This is a political book about the Boy Scouts. You'd think that the Boy Scouts were a symbol for some larger issues, but no, in fact, it's just about the Boy Scouts of America (BSA), and the troubles they have had excluding girls, gays, and godlessness over the years. Gov. Rick Perry was an Eagle Scout, the highest level of Boy Scout (calling it "the greatest extracurricular constant for most of us boys," p. 17), and defends the Boy Scouts as symbolic of everything good about American values.

Yes, there is a larger issue: the "Culture War," but Perry only extends the book's concepts to the larger issue in one slim chapter ("Taking Inventory of Society," pp. 171-178). That chapter begins, "Is American society going to hell in a handbasket?," which sums up Perry's attitude in the rest of the book, too. Excluding gays and godlessness is the real political issue—although excluding girls brought some lawsuits too—and Perry's theme revolves around how those exclusions hurt the boys involved and hurt America.

The lawsuits against BSA regarding gays and godlessness constitute the primary political issue. Perry details these lawsuits as a long-term plan of the ACLU, the American Civil Liberties Union, to promote gay rights and atheism. The book serves as an outline of how to beat the ACLU in future court battles.

On the positive side, Perry details the values that Boy Scouting promotes. These values strengthen American values, according to Perry, and hence we should all support Scouting:

- "Boy Scouts keep score" (measure success, not just effort, p. 34)

- "Be Prepared" (the Scout motto, p. 26)

- "Do a good turn daily" (the Scout slogan, p. 26)

- "They Didn't Forget the Girls" (the co-founding of the Girl Scouts, p. 42)

- "On my honor I will do my best to do my duty to God and my country" (the Scout oath, p. 45)

Perry indicates nothing in this book about running for President. It was written while Perry was governor of Texas, in the waning months of the presidential reign of the previous Governor of Texas. Perry's purpose in this book seems more to establish his Christian conservative credentials—he keeps his policy prescriptions out, detailing those in his newer book *Fed Up*. Of course, Perry knew in 2008 that establishing his Christian conservative credentials would become essential to the 2011-2012 primary, and this book accomplishes that purpose in a relevant and interesting way. For voters seeking to understand Perry as a presidential candidate, this book provides a solid underpinning.

Book review written Aug. 2011;
full excerpts available online at: www.ontheissues.org/On_My_Honor.htm

Romney vs. Perry on VoteMatch

VoteMatch is our 20-question quiz that summarizes the candidate's views on the controversial issues of the day.

VoteMatch Social Issues

	Romney	Perry
Abortion is a woman's right	opposes	strongly opposes
Require companies to hire more women & minorities	strongly favors	neutral
Same-sex domestic partnership benefits	opposes	strongly opposes
Teacher-led prayer in public schools	strongly favors	strongly favors
Parents choose schools via vouchers	strongly favors	favors

VoteMatch Domestic Issues

	Romney	Perry
More federal funding for health coverage	favors	strongly opposes
Death penalty	strongly favors	strongly favors
Mandatory Three Strikes sentencing laws	strongly favors	favors
Absolute right to gun ownership	opposes	strongly favors
Drug use is immoral: enforce laws against it	strongly favors	favors

VoteMatch Economic Issues

	Romney	Perry
Privatize Social Security	strongly favors	favors
Make taxes more progressive	strongly opposes	strongly opposes
Stricter limits on political campaign funds	opposes	opposes
Allow churches to provide welfare services	favors	favors
Replace coal & oil: with alternatives	opposes	opposes

VoteMatch International Issues

	Romney	Perry
Illegal immigrants earn citizenship	opposes	neutral
Support & expand free trade	neutral	favors
The Patriot Act harms civil liberties	strongly opposes	strongly opposes
Expand the armed forces	strongly favors	strongly favors
US out of Iraq and Afghanistan	strongly opposes	strongly opposes

In our online quiz, you fill in your answers for these 20 questions, and we match you against all the candidates. Please see: http://quiz.ontheissues.org/

Afterword

We hope that this book encourages you, as voters, to make your decisions based on the issues. We recognize the reality of American politics: voters make their decisions based primarily on whether they like the candidates. Accordingly, our goal is to get voters to compare their issue preferences in comparison to candidate issue stances when considering which candidates to like.

We intentionally omitted from this book any biographical background on Gov. Romney and Gov. Perry. Details of their birthplaces and religious affiliations—and minutiae of every other personal detail—are readily available in the mainstream media. Their issue stances are more challenging for voters to find.

Why does the mainstream media fail at this important function? Because they are "news" organizations which are poorly suited to covering political campaigns. "News" implies reporting on what is "new": Romney's stance on school prayer has not changed since 1994, and Perry's stance on gays in the Boy Scouts has not changed since 2007, so there's nothing in the news about those issues. But if you are impassioned about school prayer, or if you vote based on gay rights policy, then you cannot rely on the news media for those non-newsworthy issues. That's where we come in.

This book represents an archive of where these two candidates stand on the key issues of our time. We don't consider whether candidates' issue stances are new—just what they say on each issue. That often requires a lot of digging on our part—we have a team of researchers to do that, but we invite you to volunteer any issue stances that we don't cover.

Our online website www.ontheissues.org covers many more issues than can fit in any book: many more stances from Romney and Perry, as well as all of the other 2012 candidates, Governors, Senators, and House members. We score each candidate on a 20-question quiz called "VoteMatch." A representation of the VoteMatch quiz results for the presidential contenders appears on the back cover of this book. The mainstream media interpret candidates using a one-dimensional "right-left" analysis. That simplistic analysis comes to nonsensical conclusions like calling Ron Paul "extreme right-wing" even though he opposes the Iraq War; opposes the PATRIOT Act; supports drug legalization; and supports same-sex domestic partnership benefits.

We find our two-dimensional analysis to be more accurate in differentiating candidates than that traditional one-dimensional analysis. We don't claim that our method is perfect—just superior to the simplistic mainstream media. VoteMatch uses a Social Issues dimension plus an Economic Issues dimension; we interpret candidates based on whether they believe in government involvement in either or both of those dimensions. Using the two-dimensional analysis differentiates five classes of political beliefs:

1. *Libertarian:*
   No government involvement in social issues
   No government involvement in economic issues

2. *Conservative:*
   Government involvement in social issues
   No government involvement in economic issues

3. *Liberal:*
   No government involvement in social issues
   Government involvement in economic issues

4. *Populist:*
   Government involvement in social issues
   Government involvement in economic issues

5. *Centrist:*
   Some government involvement in social issues
   Some government involvement in economic issues

Most importantly, you can answer the same 20 questions and see *your* political label and how the candidates match up with *you*. We invite you to try the VoteMatch quiz at:

http://quiz.ontheissues.org

Other Books in This Series

- Obama vs. Hillary Clinton On The Issues

- Palin vs. Bachmann On The Issues

- Ron Paul vs. Gary Johnson On The Issues

- Michele Bachmann vs. Rick Santorum On The Issues

- Ron Paul vs. Rick Santorum On The Issues

About the Author

JESSE GORDON has been the editor-in-chief of OnTheIssues.org since its formation in 1999. His passion revolves around providing issue-based coverage on political races, to combat the mainstream media's growing lack of such coverage.

Mr. Gordon holds a Master's degree in Public Policy from Harvard University's Kennedy School of Government. He and the website OnTheIssues.org are based in Cambridge, Massachusetts. He resides with his fiancée, Kathleen; his son, Julien; Kathleen's son, Derek; their cat, Chanel; and six fish with whom Chanel is obsessed.

Mr. Gordon replies to email personally, at jesse@ontheissues. org—whether to suggest improvements to the website or to order one of the other books above.